DOING BUSINESS IN BRAZIL
OPPORTUNITIES AND THREATS

Isabella M. P. de Vasconcellos

Isabellavasconcellos@terra.com.br

PHD candidate Business – ESC- École Supérieure de Commerce, Rennes – France. MBA Marketing – Loyola University of Chicago - Graduate School of Business Chicago – USA. Master in Business Administration – Fundação Getúlio Vargas, Rio de Janeiro – Brazil.

Consultant and Professor. Professional Experience in Marketing, Sales, Partnership Development and Strategy Planning in major companies. Development of In-Company Training Programs for Marketing / Product Managers and Sales Force.

Contents:

Introduction

Brazil is a huge country in terms of geography, population and business opportunities.

On the other hand, it is a victim of poor public management that has not been able to reduce taxes, promote long-term development and invest adequately in education and infrastructure to reduce the necessity for expenditures in social programs.

The country has been recently in the spotlight due to disclosure of cases of corruption involving politicians, executives and the largest corporation in Brazil: Petrobras, the state-owned oil company.

This has also brought major impacts on the political and economic framework, causing recession and unemployment throughout the whole business value chain.

However, it is still a country of opportunities for those able to manage the challenges.

Mr. Rob Arnott, founder and CEO of Research Affiliates in an investment analysis stated that the big difference between developed and emerging countries is their demography. He related the macroeconomic growth to the age of the population. Countries where the greatest part of the population is between 40 and 60 years old can strongly contribute to the GNP- Gross National Product. On the other hand, only in countries where the majority of the population is made up of young adults can provide productivity increase and strongly contribute to GNP growth.

In the next thirty years, 80% of the total world population will be outside of Europe and USA, which means that investing in emerging countries will be the best long-term growth strategy. The world's emerging economies are living their best moment: the average age of their population is around 30 while in developed countries it is 43. Those emerging countries can offer great investment opportunities, but this demands confident and patient investors. Brazil is part of this promising group of countries.

In 2001, Jim O'Neil coined the term BRIC to denote a group of four countries (Brazil, Russia, India and China). They were all populous nations and ambitious in their economies and, at that time, represented only 8% of the total world economy. Ten years later their share of the world economy had jumped to 20%. Many economists, even Brazilians, questioned if Brazil should have been included in that promising group.

At the same time that the global crisis in 2008 closed 62 million jobs according to data from the International Labor Organization, 10.5 million new job opportunities were created in Brazil.

Brazil is among the eight countries in G-20 group and ranked seventh in terms of GNP with US$ 2.2 trillion in 2013, a 63% increase over a period of five years. International trade increased 23% over the same period. Agricultural production doubled and the country became one of the most dynamic and modern world players as leading exporter of sugar, coffee, soybeans, corn, beef and chicken.

Brazil has a solid financial system and expanded the amount of local credit from US$ 140 billion to US$ 1 trillion in eleven years, maintaining the same level of guarantees. This brought poor people into the economy removing 36 million Brazilian out of poverty and adding some 42 million to the middle class, reducing social inequality.

Some fifteen million people in rural areas were given access to electricity for the first time and three million families received government-built homes. Supported by the social programs, seven million new students were able to enroll in undergraduate courses and sixty thousand students were sent to study abroad.

This social inclusion program brought new opportunities for consumption in different areas. Brazil went from being a vulnerable country to an international competitor and is now ranked among the first five destinations for foreign direct investment.

After four years of economic and income growth, efforts by the federal government to obtain reelection brought on an unsettled period of economic instability. Government spending exceeded tax revenues and public investment was reduced to offset the fiscal shortfall, while taxes, already high, were raised even further on many products and economic activities. The country is currently in the midst of a recession and the government is working to reestablish fiscal balance by cutting spending, reducing tax incentives and raising taxes in general. It currently faces strong political opposition and charges of corruption, which have weakened its ability to progress. Nonetheless, there appears to be a move in the right direction.

Although the country is in the middle of what appears to be a transient and manageable crisis, companies are looking for new sources of growth in the face of increasing global competition. Brazil has a large local potential market, which is important for many companies.

In the last eleven years, the federal government has created and implemented a social program known as "*Bolsa Família*". It works as financial aid to combat poverty and promote social inclusion. The program assists 14 million families and 36 million people have left the level of absolute poverty. The program has been recognized internationally for its success. Families receive approximately US$ 55 monthly and, at same time, their children need to attend school and maintain an attendance percentage of 85% confirmed by an audit done every two months. More than 96% of the 15.7 million students monitored by the system are meeting this requirement to maintain the benefit. In addition, they must comply with the national vaccination calendar program. Higher education is fundamental to raise productivity in the Brazilian economy. The program assists twenty-five per cent of the country's poorest residents. It costs 0.5% of the GNP and the spending has generated returns to stimulate the economy.

To be successful, companies need to be able to apply local marketing strategy in emerging markets and develop and implement the proper strategies for sales and distribution, communication, pricing, product lines, etc. Companies' challenges to conduct business in different countries are related to addressing variations in key marketing capabilities and obtaining local customer insights. It is necessary to be aware of unique local conditions and many marketers have been able to transfer learning from developing to developed markets.

This book gives an overview of different sectors of the economy where there are business opportunities and threats.

An Overview of Brazil
The potential consumer market

Today Brazil represents a consumer market of 210 million people, a great opportunity for many kinds of business. It is the fifth most populous country in world. On the other hand, per capita GDP is still very low: approximately $12,000, equivalent to 22% of the U.S. However, this has not prevented Brazil from becoming the world's largest consumer market for perfumes, second largest for hair treatment products, third for cosmetics and soft drinks and the fourth for bottled water, not to mention many other products like chocolate, mobile phones, video games, wall tiles and automobiles.

One important issue that has attracted investors to the country is the maturity level of the consumers' consumption basket. In other words, while many consumer items already exist in American and European homes, they do not exist in many of the sixty million Brazilian houses. Some examples of that are: computers, refrigerators, ovens, washing machines, tablets and many other consumer products and services like cable TV, fixed and mobile internet. That fact represents a great opportunity for new business. Approximately twenty million houses still require a large variety of home appliances.

As Svein Harald Oygrad, partner of McKinsey & Company and ex-Finance Minister in Norway said, Brazil is the country where the consumer product industry must be to invest and grow. Bruce Andrews, American sub-secretary of commerce also stated that American companies view Brazil as a great market opportunity.

Unilever is planning to invest US$ 250 million to expand its local production of deodorant, the world's largest consumer market where average per capita annual sales is US$ 24, higher than Australia (US$ 16), USA (US$ 12) and South Africa (US$ 8). In fact, Brazil is the second largest market for Unilever after USA.

Companies like Subway, Dunkin Donuts, Hooters, McDonald's, Johnny Rockets, Sbarro, Outback and Domino's are among the large chains opening new stores in Brazil. In fact, the economy slowdown has been attracting new franchisers, due to more favorable rent conditions and greater availability of good locations. The opportunity is to focus on the middle class of one hundred million people. As

2.3 million Brazilians visited USA in 2014, they are very familiar with those brands.

There are also important opportunities in the education area. British Group Pearson, who sold Financial Times and the Economist, has decided to invest in emerging countries and Brazil is top on their list. Pearson products and services are marketed locally and it has five million students from the elementary school to the college level. With an investment of US$ 700 million, Pearson acquired some educational groups to meet the growing demand in the market for better qualified manpower.

Another business opportunity involves highest-income consumers, who represent 10% of the population. This segment is responsible for 41.2% of the country's income and they are consumers of luxury items.

Creating a powerful emerging-market strategy has moved to the top of growth agendas of many multinational companies (Atsmon, 2011). Brazil's diversity and dynamism defy any one-size-fits-all approach. It is necessary to plan by targeting city clusters within the country, and companies can seize growth opportunities. To do that, business models must be reviewed and new organizational forms and value chains included in order to drive wealth creation. Business model design indeed is central to value creation (Zott and Amit, 2013).

New markets typically offer challenges and risks in linking transnational companies to distinctive cultural resources and companies have difficulty in defining the right product portfolio, distribution and price strategies, which need to be tailored to local characteristics. Strategy means choosing a set of activities to deliver a unique mix of value (Kotler, 1996). These activities may include efficiency in operational process, technological tools, positioning and human resources to achieve sustainable profitability. '

Strategy cannot be considered flat and stable. Instead, it needs to be adjusted based on market conditions, customer needs or accessibility. UNILEVER launched an economical and larger laundry package in Brazil, targeting higher-income consumers and, during the same period, was forced to reduce the package size of the same product in Europe, to serve unemployed consumers in the midst of the region's economic crises.

In this era of market saturation in developed economies and the increasing quest for globalization, companies are looking for ways to leverage opportunities in new and emerging markets (Morh and Arnould, 2005). Some three billion consumers from the developing world will have joined the middle class by 2030 (Nguyen et al., 2014). In Latin America, Brazil's growth will contribute to business development, offering many opportunities as well as challenges related to macroeconomic and social constraints.

Competitiveness in today's global world requires business organizations to develop strategies and processes that are both economically competitive and socially responsible (Stead, 2013). Sometimes it becomes essential to develop partnerships with local players to strengthen existing business opportunities.

This book brings comparative case studies discussing strategies used by some multinational companies in Brazil and shows the critical factors they had to face. These companies created their own ways to address unique regional characteristics and succeeded in formulating and executing their strategies to support domestic growth.

Variables intrinsic to opportunities and risks that are present in developing countries like Brazil were also considered and reports included some successful experiences by companies like NESTLE, COCA-COLA, and DANONE. These companies had to work either on their local business models, pricing or commercial and logistics strategies or on product and communication strategies. The objective here is to provide guidance in identifying unique local characteristics and potential business opportunities, referring to real cases of strategies, which made Brazilian operations vibrant and market-driven.

Strategies have shifted from manufacturing productivity to market and customer approach issues such as product differentiation and capillarity.

Strategic Planning goes beyond analysis of opportunities and threats. Strategic marketing management addresses four questions: how, what, when and to whom the firm should target its marketing effort. It also needs to find how to ensure long-run profitability and growth. A strategic error can threaten a company's survival. As Jim Collins (2002) said, business must be built to last. Targeting the right consumer and defining the right suppliers are part of the plan.

Attention now turns to the fundamental aspect of the regional market and underlying rationale for the strategy. Increasing change in the business environment leads to more flexible, innovation-driven organizational structures and processes. As Barney (1991) stated, strategic planning demands strategic management, which is a continuous process involving the efforts of top management to react to environmental, social, demographic and economic change. The essence of strategy is selecting one market position that a company can claim as its own and unique.

Geographic, Economic and Demographic Data

It is important to provide guidance in identifying local peculiarities and potential business opportunities, referring to real cases of strategy that transformed operations in Brazil into vibrant market-driven organizations. In other words, the key issues are to understand how and what to do in such a huge market.

It is important to establish a managerial process to maintain a fit between the organization's objectives, its resources and the ever-changing market opportunities. In addition, the existence of different regional cultures and low educational level can be most effectively overcome by adopting the right strategy.

Despite the economic growth driven by private and public investments, there are still numerous obstacles to overcome.

Brazil's population is larger than the populations of Italy, Spain and France combined. It represents a great opportunity for many kinds of businesses. Although its per capita GDP is still very low, it has not been an obstacle to the country becoming the world's largest consumer market for perfumes, hair treatment products, cosmetics and soft drinks. São Paulo, Brazil's largest city has more helicopters than New York City. The fashion market in Brazil has increased 287% over the last decade, more than China and Russia, which increased 261% and 200% respectively over the same period (Euro monitor report).

As a first step in strategy, companies need to identify possible market segments to direct their marketing efforts. In Brazil, different social classes can mean different and profitable business opportunities. The dominant class C, or middle class, is the largest one with approximately one hundred million people. They have an average family income of US$ 20,800. This group shares the same behavioral norms and is eager to expand consumption, although average income is very low. Its consumption is based on financing and tax incentives, which have been strongly motivated by governmental banks. Therefore, the real estate, home appliance, furniture and automotive industries have had a period of significant growth.

A wage increase has occurred in the country due to a low unemployment rate (6%) over the last four years and brought about some changes in consumption habits.

On the other hand, total income is still very concentrated and only ten per cent of the population accounts for 41.2% of total income.

One of the more intriguing aspects of this analysis, for example, is understanding how such a low-income country can be so attractive to many industries, even for those in the luxury business.

A good example would be the premium beer market.in Brazil. The country is positioned as the world' third largest beer market. An increasing premium segment represents today only 5% to 6% of total Brazilian beer consumption while in countries like the U.S. it is 15%. As income has increased, consumers have become willing to pay for sophisticated products.

On the other hand, the "A" and "B" social classes, the upper and upper middle classes, comprise the segment of wealthy Brazilians of approximately fifty million people. In terms of consumer buying patterns, the affluent are more likely to own their homes, purchase new cars and consume luxury brands intensively.

The most famous international luxury brands have stores in the city of São Paulo, with a population of 17 million, in Brazil's Southeast region.

While the country's population has been growing at an average annual rate of 0.8%, the North and Central West regions have been growing at over 3.5% a year, indicating a strong tendency for migration. In fact, 39% of all Brazilians do not live in the same city in which they were born.

The aging of the Brazilian population is a fact and 23% of the population is over age 50. Only 39.6% of the population is under age 24. This is increasing the demand for new products such as health supplements, tour packages, computer courses and many other kinds of entertainment.

Another important consideration in product development and communication strategy is racial distribution. Overall, 46.2 % of the population is white meaning that more than half of the people have some degree of African descent. This balance varies dramatically in some regions: while in the South, 76.8% of the population is white, in the North this percentage drops to 22%. Some companies like "Beleza Natural Institute", a hair dresser for African descent people, has proven to be a successful case offering different products, especially for hair and skin treatment. In twenty years, the Institute reached US$100 million in annual revenues serving 100,000 customers a month in four different Brazilian states. Its manufacturing plant produces 270 tons per month of 50 different products.

Another issue is the low level of education. 8.7% of the population is illiterate and 18.3% have less than four years of schooling. Despite this disadvantage, they are consumers. Unilever has developed a specific laundry soap product for this segment and the brand name had only three huge letters, "ALA", priced at under the equivalent of US$ 0.50. The company followed Mc Donald's principle that uses its big yellow "M" to be identified even by small children who are not able to read.

As average income increases, the demand for private schools also increases as a consequence of the shortage of good public schools. Around fifty million children are at school age from kindergarten to high school. There are forty thousand private schools in Brazil and they obtained US$ 23.96 billion in revenues in 2012, with an enrollment of 16.6 million students. National and international groups are present in this activity, which accounts for 1.5% of the GNP. Day care, basic education and high school are the most demanding services. To meet this expanding and urgent demand, specialists say that an appropriate business model needs to be developed to be able to offer monthly tuition between US$ 185 and US$ 333. While at the university level, the private sector runs institutions responsible for 74% of enrollment, in basic education its share is only 22% (9 million students). Social classes C and D (the middle and lower middle class respectively) are the segments with the highest demand.

The educational market has evolved significantly. On average, educational institution net profit margin was 17.7% and return on equity was 15.1% during this period. The accelerated process of mergers and acquisitions brought some gains in synergy related to suppliers and marketing expenses.

For university students there is a student loan program (Fies) sponsored by the federal government that allowed 5.14 million students to enroll in 2,112 private universities. Brazil has 5,570 municipalities, but only 63 federal universities. The private sector is responsible for meeting the market demand.

Although the private sector has a strong participation at the undergraduate level, there is still a potential market for investors. Only 17.8% of young people between 18 and 24 years are enrolled in college-level programs. Besides that, the market demand for qualified labor is increasing.

In the same scenario, opportunities for e-learning are tremendous and distance learning education has emerged as an alternative in a growing market like Brazil with almost

210 million people, where it has become a vital strategy in the ongoing educational process. The significant growth of this form of education in the country has taken place at universities in regular full undergraduate courses, in graduate courses or in specific short-term specialization programs. The demand for new courses has increased and many educational institutions have also developed distance learning for non-formal and corporate courses for their personnel development.

There are 5,570 cities in Brazil and most of them (82%) have populations over less than fifty thousand. That means many kinds of business would not achieve their breakeven point in those cities, including retail stores, private schools, extended learning courses and universities.

This internet access is subsidized by the federal government. Domestic improvements made in internet availability have also contributed to the increase of this form of education. In October/2016 (http://www.teleco.com.br/3g_cobertura.asp), 3G broadband was already available in 87. 6% of the cities where 97. 5% of the population live. Besides that, the large number of young people who want to navigate on the internet may also help spur interest for this kind of course.

There is an increase of students interested in this type of education. According to the Map of College Education issued by Semesp in 2012, the demand for online courses increased 12.5% while demand for onsite courses increased 6.4% over the same one-year period.

The 2015 Brazilian Census for Distance Learning accounted for 5,048,912 students. Of these, 1,108,021 were in accredited full distance learning and blended courses, 3,940,891 in corporate or non-corporate open courses. There were 1,180,296 more students enrolled than in 2014 (Censo EAD 2015).

That certainly encourages the development of experiments in this type of courses in different areas. There are 2,377 institutions in Brazil offering 29,507 different online courses and 74% belong to the private sector. The country is experiencing the situation where distance learning growth rates exceed economic growth.

Technological development has brought new business opportunities. E-Commerce is growing twenty-five percent a year and many companies have received international private equity investment. Sephora, a leading French chain of perfume and cosmetics stores, entered the

Brazilian market buying a well-known online store called Sack's. After this successful experience Sephora opened its first Brazilian retail brick-and-mortar outlet and plans to open an additional 39 stores in the country over the next five years.

As seventeen percent of population lives alone, the industry has begun to offer food in smaller packages, frozen foods and many more "ready-to-go" items.

Companies can either focus on middle class or work on a kind of business to serve the upper class segment. Selecting which alternative to pursue depends on the company's overall philosophy and culture.

Many international investors have entered the Brazilian market directly, acquiring companies in the health industry, consumer & retail, logistics or as private equity investors.

The Challenges of Taxes in Brazil

The tax burden in Brazil corresponds to 36% of GNP. Brazil is ranked in the second highest position in terms of percentage of total tax revenues to GDP in South America. Its percentage is also higher than the average tax burden in the OECD - Organization for Economic Co-operation and Development countries of 34.1%.

Tax burdens and revenue collections in advanced economies are reaching record levels according to OECD and tax composition continue with wide variations among countries. According to the Organization, in 2013, tax burden rose in 21 of the 30 countries for which data is available, and fell in the remaining nine.

The largest increases in 2013 occurred in Portugal, Turkey, the Slovak Republic, Denmark and Finland. The largest drops were in Norway, Chile and New Zealand.

In Brazil, the national tax structure was established in the Constitution, which determines that the Federal Government, States, Federal District and Municipalities can levy taxes.

The Constitution gives the right to every level of government to institute taxes, fees (corresponding to utilization of public services) and contributions designed to fund specific government activities or programs.

There are more than eighty taxes, fees and contributions in Brazil, making tax consulting a must in most businesses. That is an important issue for local business development and foreign investors who need to be aware of tax implications in their activities.

Some of the most important taxes are: Federal Income Tax (IR), Industrial Products Tax (IPI), Imports (II), Social Security, Social Contributions (CSLL, PIS, COFINS), Financial Transactions (IOF), State Taxes (ICMS-Value Added Tax), IPVA- Vehicle Ownership Tax and others) and Municipal Taxes (ISS-Service Tax, IPTU-Urban Property Tax and others).

Resident companies are taxed on worldwide income. A foreign company operating locally is subject to Brazilian taxation. The basic income tax applies to operating profits derived by companies in Brazil.

Business Opportunities and Challenges
The Dynamism that comes from the Countryside

Brazilian agribusiness exports reached the amount of US$ 95 billion (40% of total exports). This makes Brazil the world's largest food exporter overall and in items such as sugar, coffee, orange, soybeans, beef and chicken.

Brazil's GDP declined 3.8% in 2015, reflecting a strong economic recession. While industrial activity dropped 6.2%, agribusiness grew 1.8% with a record grain harvest of 202 million tons.

Due to this focus on agribusiness, new agricultural areas have been developed, leading to population migration and economic growth to new regions.

The Central West Region, the main grain producing area with 13.3 million hectares planted and 46.7 million tons of annual production as well as the North Region are the areas which are most benefitting from this trend. Although Brazil's annual grain production of 193.6 million tons is expected to increase in the coming years, there is still a major bottleneck in the logistics infrastructure, offering great opportunities for investment.

Moreover, transportation, storage, machinery and intermodal terminals have begun to be successfully operated by private investors to mitigate the deficiency in infrastructure. While in USA 60% of the harvest volume passes through producer warehouses, in Brazil this figure is only 15%, which causes an overload in the transport system and raises operating costs. Agribusiness represents 25% of Brazil's GNP and logistics costs are 4.4% of GNP. American and Japonese investors are working on integration of production, storage, truck offloading and ship loading facilities at Brazilian ports.

As agricultural land is becoming a scarce asset around the world and the growing population demands more and more proteins in emerging countries, land prices have been increasing. Land values have increased 56% in the Southeast and 92% in the Central West Region over the last three years.

If world population increases from 7 billion to 10 billion by 2050, demand for food will increase by 70% favoring countries with large agricultural areas. In Brazil, due to climate conditions, there can be up to three harvests a year vs. only one in the U.S.

Currently, Brazilian legislation does not allow foreign investors to acquire agricultural land, unless the company has majority Brazilian ownership.

New technologies have helped farmers raise productivity in areas with good topography, stable climate where the periods of rainfall are well distributed throughout the year and land is relatively inexpensive.

Brazil is the fourth largest global fertilizer consumer of NPK (nitrogen, phosphorus and potassium) macronutrients used on most farm land. Inputs for the agricultural market had record sales. Fertilizer consumption was 32.5 million tons in 2013. The bad news is that the country depends on imports to meet 80% of its domestic demand and the product is essential to guarantee the harvest. This is another possible area of investment considering the existing local demand.

The expansion of the feed and animal nutrient market to 65 million tons is supported by the need to supply poultry and pork producers who increased the productivity of their animals.

It is also a good moment for equipment producers like Massey Ferguson, Valtra and John Deere. Together, in one year, they sold more than one thousand units.

Agricultural science has also been driven by the convergence of biotechnology, geotechnology, robotics and automation. All of them are working together to expand production, while ensuring environment safety. Specialists say that it is possible to grow without deforestation.

Agribusiness has brought income and economic growth to the countryside. New developing business centers are attracting qualified labor force, new retail outlets and other related activities. Companies are working to increase international trade and expand the domestic market.

Infrastructure – Opportunities for New Business

Brazil has to accelerate investment in power generation, transportation and sanitation.

There is a strong demand to develop new logistics routes based on the extension of railroad and port infrastructure. Many products depend on them for transportation such as: iron ore, cement, steel products, coke, soybeans, fertilizers and petroleum derivatives. There is an opportunity for local producers to save 30% in freight costs vs. highways transportation heavily used today.

New projects have been stimulated by the federal law enacted in 2004, which established public and private partnerships for this type of investment. Private investors receive tax incentives and revenue from users during a concession period, to help ensure return on their investment. This business model also applies to the construction of hospitals, prisons, roads, sanitation projects, public illumination, airports and other priority areas defined by the federal, state and municipal governments.

Specialists say Brazil has only one third of the infrastructure it needs to support its economic growth.

Other investments are targeted to technological areas: The international energy agency estimates that Brazil has 245 trillion cubic feet of non-conventional gas that can be extracted from "sweet spots" (concentrations of gas and oil inside bedrock).

Energy

The energy market in Brazil is one of the most promising in world due to its urgent demand and need for heavy investment. The Government forecasts an investment of R$ 150 billion (US$ 55 billion) over the next five years focused on power generation and transmission. Equipment suppliers and companies specialized in this sector will have to overcome some challenges.

Today the energy matrix is concentrated on oil, sugarcane and hydropower.

ENERGY MATRIX	
SOURCE	% OF CONSUMPTION
Oil and derivatives	38.5
Sugarcane and derivatives	17.7
Hydropower	14.2
Natural Gas	10.2
Firewood and charcoal	9.5
Coal and derivatives	5.1
Renewable sources	3.4
Uranium	1.4

In the sugar and alcohol sector, second generation ethanol plants are ready to begin operation, creating a new cycle for this industry. Large companies like Petrobras, Odebrecht and Granbio are investing in a project of "second generation sugarcane" to produce cellulosic ethanol. While the first generation produces 83 liters of ethanol per ton of dried biomass, second-generation ethanol plants will produce 270 to 300 liters from the same amount of biomass. In this process, the sugar from cellulose extracted from sugarcane bagasse is converted into ethanol. Today, approximately 65% per cent of the car fleet runs on ethanol; as the third largest producer of biodiesel, the country has a great growth potential leveraged by exports to the European market.

With the drop in oil prices in the international market, investments in sugar and alcohol sector and also in pre-salt layer oil exploration have been affected and are being reevaluated. Therefore, at the moment, investors are not focused on the construction of new ethanol plants but are investing US$ 5 billion to acquire new equipment, technology, harvest and planting mechanization and logistics to increase productivity to achieve production of 7.1 thousand liters of sugarcane ethanol per hectare. In the U.S., using corn, productivity is 3.2 thousand liters per hectare. In ten years, Brazilian sugarcane has doubled and total installed capacity is 700 million tons of ethanol.

By 2023, Brazil has the objective to double oil production to five million barrels per day exploring the pre-salt layer, which would place it among the world's five largest producers.

This set of opportunities also brings some challenges. As 45% of energy comes from renewable sources, investments need to conciliate economic growth and environmental conservation to expand power generation and the greatest potential is precisely in the Amazon region. In the North Region, restrictions related to indigenous areas have also delayed some projects.

The supply of electrical power is also expected to increase by more than 63 thousand megawatts over the next ten years. Two very large hydroelectric plants are under construction: Belo Monte (that will be the third largest in world) and São Luiz do Tapajós that will supply energy to fifteen million people in the North Region. Along with that increase in power generation, transmission and distribution, new business opportunities will be created.

The country's potential for wind farms and solar power opportunities is enormous. The combination of natural resources like nearly year round sunshine, constant coastal wind and many waterfalls can offer the country the opportunity to double its generating capacity over the next five years. Alternative energy sources may represent promising business opportunities.

Current hydropower plants are being built without large reservoirs, known as "run-of-the-river". This means that these plants offer a low level of stored energy, which can be risky during periods of heavy drought such as the one the country faced last year.

On the other hand, construction of hydroelectric power plants close to the large cities lowers the cost of installing long transmission lines.

Today hydropower plants account for 80% of total Brazilian electric power consumption. Roughly thirty five per cent of its potential has already been explored. The other sixty-five per cent are located in Amazon region, which increases the marginal cost of hydroelectric expansion. The construction of a 10,500 km electrical transmission network and 21 substations in this region will serve the existing demand and the projected annual growth forecast of 4.9% for the coming years.

The recent threat of energy shortage demanded investments in new alternatives for the energy matrix. Thermal power plants have been frequently activated increasing the price of energy due to their higher cost. In fact, specialists say the country needs to double the number of thermal power plants, but to be more efficient and less costly, they should run on natural gas. Government has bid new thermal power plants based on the use of biomass, natural gas and coal.

The first auction for solar energy took place in 2014 when it represented only 1.5% of energy supply (included among renewable sources). The market expects that, in the next three decades, it may supply as much as 13% of total residential demand. Its price is still not yet competitive, but new government policies are attracting new investors.

However, due to its variability, consumers cannot count on solar energy during the hours of peak consumption, so thermal power plants are still necessary and they depend on the availability of natural gas. These plants are responsible for 25% of total energy consumption and gas shortage limits new investments. Diesel is the other fuel option.

There are more than 250 Eolic energy plants in operation and 411 more are under construction. They will be ready to produce energy by 2019. By 2016, a total installed capacity of fourteen thousand MW is expected. Today it represents 3.3% of the energy matrix and government policy intends to raise it to 5.5% by 2017. The country is ranked tenth in terms of installed capacity and it produces the most inexpensive Eolic energy in world. There are strong, constant and unidirectional winds in the north and northeast regions of the country, but consumption is mostly concentrated in the southeast. That demands a huge investment in electric transmission network. As the economy in Europe has slowed down, many international suppliers have focused on Brazil and equipment prices have dropped.

All these initiatives are aimed at implementing a government program known as "Light for Everyone" ("*Luz para Todos*"). This program has reached almost fifty million people in rural areas and generated more than four hundred thousand new job positions. It was also reflected on the sales of home appliances, since 79% of the beneficiaries recently bought their first TV sets and refrigerators.

Telecommunications

Telecommunications has become a large scale business and business concentration has been promoted by recent acquisitions. In the first half of 2016, there were some 271.1 million mobile phones for a population of 210 million people. Although it may seem like a mature market, in fact, mobile service is going through innovation and creating new business opportunities like M2M – machine-to-machine communications. Analyzing this more carefully, only 62% of them are smartphones (www.anatel.gov.br). Smartphones and tablets devices represent 83% of total internet connection volume

Telecom operators invested US$ 150 billion in Brazil in the last fifteen years, to expand infrastructure and increase product and service portfolio. Among new solutions the market demands communication between on-board car computers to insurance companies; electronic home appliances connected to household mobile phones; management of truck fleets to track cargo; and management of bus routes to inform passengers waiting time until the next bus. There are still plenty of development opportunities to explore considering that today 64% of mobile phones are pre-paid, with limited services.

Communication needs in the South and Southeast regions have been fully met. On the other hand, the North and Central West regions are still not fully covered by telecommunication service. One of the reasons for that is the precarious condition of access and infrastructure available, making some investments risky.

Public phones covered by river flood

Load Transportation

Today the Brazilian freight transportation mode matrix is unbalanced. Highways are used to transport 60% of products manufactured in the country (25 million tons). They are also used for 90% of passenger transportation. The amount transported is expected to grow to 120 million tons by 2031.

Most of the roads (88%) are simple one-lane highways with no shoulders. Most of them are deficient in some aspect such as pavement, signage or engineering.

The number of cars and trucks traveling on highways has increased due to the

development of new industrial centers in the North and Central West regions. Those areas demand urgent infrastructure improvements as they account for the bulk of the country's sugar, soy, wheat, corn, cotton and meat production. These highways have excessive truck traffic, leading to high freight costs and harm the environment.

To meet this demand some 6,800 km of roads are in the bidding process and public-private sector partnerships are being promoted to leverage the investment.

Some companies have made their own investments in transportation infrastructure. An example is Bunge, the agribusiness giant that is using the Tapajós-Amazon River Waterway as an export route.

This initiative is expected to reduce the transportation cost by 30%. Today 85% of total production of the Midwest has to be sent to Port of Santos in Southeast region. After the Port of Itaqui in the North region opens the distance between Brazil and Japan will be 25% shorter. The agricultural production of this region will be loaded in this new port using combined transportation (waterways, roads and railways) and this will generate 10% additional revenue to soy producers and 20% to corn producers.

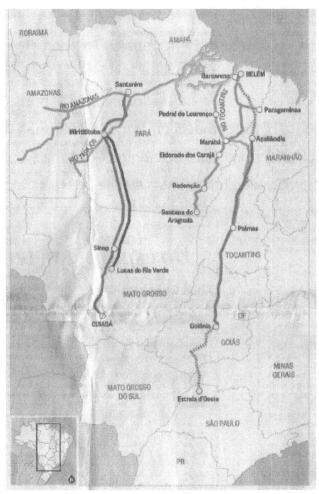

Figure 1: Port of Itaqui route

Source: O Globo 03/14/2016

Railways

New investments in eleven thousand kilometers of railways and 270 regional airports are also projected to help meet the demand from the increase in agricultural production. This railway expansion aims to link ten different states and improve the flow of iron ore and grains. Iron ore and coal represent 75.71% of total cargo hauled and agribusiness production another 14.8%. Some 159 new areas are being opened at Brazilian ports to receive this agricultural production, some of which in partnership with the private sector.

According KPMG in a partnership with Mowat Centre from Canada, government policies must be focused on this tripod to become competitive (*Anuário Exame-infraestrutura*/2014-2015): accelerated urbanization, global commerce integration and increasing pressure on the preservation of natural resources.

In addition, the federal government is bidding the construction of some 11,500 km of track for 16 railroads, representing an investment of US$ 33.7 billion.

Central Western producers depend on trucks to ship production. Most of it is sent to the ports in the southeast region. A new rail route is under construction to allow production to be shipped using ports in the North region, which is much closer, reducing freight costs by 30%.

The PPP- Public and Private Partnership Program has been implemented with 21 companies and consortia in 71 different projects of new railroad tracks.

Brazil's rail network is small, only 31,000 kilometers, vs. 225,000 kilometers in the USA and 30,000 in France, a much smaller country. While in Canada and USA 46% of cargo is transported by rail, in Brazil this percentage is only 28%.

Airports

The number of passengers transported by air has tripled in the last ten years to 111 million and is expected to double by 2022. To meet this increasing demand, the five largest airports in Brazil, responsible for 45% of total traffic, have been privatized. Viracopos Airport in Campinas-SP, responsible for 70% of Brazil's total air cargo, is now managed by a joint venture between three companies: Triunfo, HTC and Egis.

There are 2527 airports and airfields and 72% are privately owned. This is still a small number for such a large country. Cities or group of cities with gross domestic product above US$ 370 million will be authorized to implement and improve their airports using the National Civil Aviation Fund (FNAC). The objective is to increase capillarity and offer consumers more routes. Approximately 197 million people travelled in 2014, on 2.8 million flights, 95% to destinations within the country. The government projects an annual demand of 600 million passengers by 2034.

Civil Construction Industry

After four years of intensive demand for building and infrastructure projects, activity declined sharply in 2015 and the downward trend is expected to continue in 2016 albeit at a slower rate. The housing deficit is 5.8 million units. Besides that, 16.6 million people pay rent or live in homes lent to them by friends or family members. This number indicates the huge potential market for new home construction.

In 2007, real estate financing represented 1.8% of the GNP. In 2014, this percentage was five times higher: 9.1%. It continues to be subsidized and uses deposits in saving accounts as the major source of funding. In 2014, US$ 46.5 billion in loans were approved. The low default rate of 1.2% has also attracted the interest of banks. Demand exceeds supply. Every year 1.3 million Brazilian families vie for 700,000 homes. The current economic recession has slowed growth, but demand continues to increase.

The federal program known as MCMV-*Minha Casa Minha Vida* (My Home, My Life) launched in 2009 focused on financing low-income homes to people at the lower end of the social pyramid. The number of properties acquired for this purpose was 3.5 million and through the end of 2014, two million homes had been delivered. In 2015, some 350,000 new contracts were signed. Each property is worth less than US$ 185,000. This remains a federal government priority as part of its social program.

Besides federal investment in this segment, state and municipal governments have invested in public and private partnerships to build new homes for needy people.

If the employment rate remains flat, this kind of demand will tend to increase as mortgage installments tends to be lower than rent on equivalent residences.

The lack of confidence in the economic situation and the proposed fiscal adjustments under study by the government has postponed investments. At the same time, a program of concessions will tend to be accelerated to guarantee infrastructure investment considered relevant to reestablish the economy growth.

According to Sobratema – the Brazilian Technical Association for Construction and Mining, the need for investment in infrastructure including mapped and planned projects amounts to US$ 440 billion through 2018. The potential market for public works and infrastructure concessions represents 8% of all world investments in the next twenty years, according to a study by KPMG Consulting. Chinese and Spanish companies have been investing during this period of uncertainty in economy growth.

On the other hand, the rate of business-related construction has slowed down. This includes the construction of commercial office space and shopping centers that ended 2014 with a high percentage of unsold property. Demand has grown for industrial warehouses and other facilities in regional centers, along highways that link the big cities to small and medium cities, which are new areas under development.

Along the value chain, manufacturers of construction inputs such as steel and concrete structures felt the effect of the recession in 2014 and 2015. They slowed investments in 2015, but are considering plans to increase production capacity in 2016 or 2017. The industry of building materials like paints and coatings as well as faucets and toilets is working focused on the demand for new popular housing sponsored by the government federal program MCMV.

Brazilian Insurance Market perspectives

The economic reforms introduced by the Brazilian government, namely the economic stabilization plan, deregulation, the opening of the market to foreign insurers and privatization had a profound impact on the insurance market, which, in the last several years evolved from 2.55% of the GNP to 7% in 2014. The expected nominal growth in 2015 is 12%. Forecasted revenues are R$ 364.8 billion (roughly equivalent to US$ 100 billion as of the end of 2015) including the segments of personal insurance (44.5%), capitalization (5.7%), private pension (3.8%) and health insurance (46%). The market remains strong and there is increasing interest from foreign investors like the French group AXE and Mitsui of Japan. Many of them are focusing on Brazil as a target for investment to take advantage of the depreciated local currency.

The Insurance market in Brazil is regulated by SUSEP - Superintendence of Private Insurance and is directly linked to Ministry of Finance. It is also responsible for supervision and control of insurance, open private pension funds and capitalization markets in Brazil. Insurers and Pension Funds are together the main institutional investors in public and private bonds responding for R$ 1.5 trillion (US$ 279 billion).

There are other authorities responsible for different segments of the insurance, reinsurance, private pension and capitalization industry as well as health insurance and PREVIC – National Superintendence of Complementary Pensions that supervises closed private pension funds.

Private pensions - As the government social security's deficit continues to grow, and more restrictions are made by the government, new laws have been stimulating public and private employees to invest in private pension plans. In four years, contributions to these plans have grown from US$ 3.03 billion to US$ 4.07 billion, a 34% increase. Private pension funds 17 million retirement accounts corresponding to a total amount of US$ 130 billion.

The Federal Government has changed the rules for public employee's retirement reducing benefits, and since then, demand for complementary private pension plans has increased. The number of people sixty years or older has increased from 7% in 2011 to 11% in 2013 and is expected to grow to 19% by 2030. That represents a potential market of forty million people. Today, the private pension sector manages 17 million pensioners and accumulated savings of US$ 130 billion, twice the amount twenty years ago. The prospects of maintaining this positive scenario is also relevant considering that these products are financial investment instruments that could be used as an alternative to the official social security program, whose reform is under continuous discussion by society.

The market supervised by SUSEP is made up of almost 160 companies, 72% of which are insurance companies, 17% entities exclusively dedicated to offering open private pension arrangements and 11% companies exclusively dedicated to offering capitalization plans. Some life insurance companies are also allowed to offer open private pension programs.

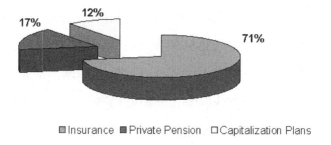

17%   12%   71%

Figure 2: Insurance Plans

Source: www.susep.org.br

Insurance premiums in Brazil are concentrated in three lines of businesses: life, automotive (including compulsory insurance for third party liability – DPVAT) and health insurance. Together they account for approximately 84% of total premium revenues.

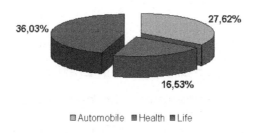

36,03%   27,62%   16,53%

Figure 3: Insurance categories

Source: www.susep.org.br

In 2003, SUSEP started a modernization process based on international standards adopted in the most developed markets, notably the IAIS Core Principles. New rules were adopted in corporate governance and internal controls, director accountability, strengthening of the roles of actuaries and auditors and employee certification.

Once a state monopoly, the reinsurance market was deregulated and opened for private investors in 2007. The Brazilian Institute of Reinsurance (IRB Brazil RE) is currently majority-owned by private companies with a minority interest still in the hands of the federal government. IRB Brazil RE in the past also accumulated regulatory responsibilities for reinsurance, coinsurance and retrocession operations and was instrumental in promoting the development of the insurance and business in the country.

Following approval of new regulations and operational guidelines, a larger portion of the risks in Brazil are expected to be reinsured by global programs. This new regulation has attracted 216 global reinsurance companies to the country. In 2012, the reinsurance market in Brazil had US$ 2 billion in assigned insurance premiums.

The increase of the new business opportunities from increased activities, introduction of new products and income increase as well as the opening of the market to foreign participants, helped enhance the performance of the industry. Foreign companies such as Liberty, Tokyo Marine, Allianz, Generalli, Chubb, Ace, Berkley and AIG are responsible for 65% of the business.

Brazil is the largest insurance market in Latin America. Current prospects point to a more mature insurance market with great growth probabilities in the near future. The effects of government policies on income distribution and social security will have a positive effect on the Brazilian insurance market.

Potential niches can be observed and explored in the Brazilian market, like micro insurance, luxury insurance, protection for small- and medium-sized companies, specific products for hotels, supermarkets, pet shops, medical and aesthetic clinics, car and life insurance and internal credit lines. There are other new opportunities in insurance for things like kidnapping, environmental issues, travel and finance.

Health Care Market

There is general level of dissatisfaction with the quality of the public health care system. In a recent survey, some 78% gave the system an unfavorable rating. This is the scenario of the Brazilian public health service used by some 160 million people who depend on it. The other 50 million are able to pay for private health insurance, but still use the public service for emergencies, vaccines and complex procedures such as transplants.

Some specialists say the main reasons for this situation are insufficient financial resources, poor management and high dependence on imported technology. Today, total government expenses with public health service represent 8.9% of GNP or US$ 40.4 billion.

Of course, it is difficult to separate health from sanitation, employment, income, education and culture. However, it is clear that the health care network service is insufficient to serve the whole population. Partnerships between public and private sectors, known as PPPs- Public and Private Partnership have been used to stimulate local production of new medication, equipment and laboratory facilities. There is an estimated demand of US$ 7 billion for local production of consumer products and equipment for labs, hospitals, radiology, dentistry and implants. Currently Brazil has to import a large portion of these items, contributing some US$ 4.9 billion to its trade deficit. The law requires all public federal hospitals to purchase equipment from national producers despite the fact that their prices are generally 8% to 15% higher than international suppliers of equivalent equipment.

Law 11.079 regulated the PPP program in 2004 but only last year was the project accelerated and investments made totaling US$ 1 billion including inauguration of four hospitals and a medication manufacturing facility. Another ten projects are underway in eight different states. The target is to improve quality of service optimizing operations and reducing costs. Finep, BNDES (the Federal Government Development Bank) and the Health Ministry have already financed US$ 4.8 billion through this partnership program. Domestic production of health care products will save the country some US$ 1.5 billion in foreign exchange. Generic drugs are also part of the research and development innovation process. Today they represent 28.2% of total sales of US$ 5.2 billion, but manufacturers are working to increase this share to 50% based on some other mature markets where market share for generic drugs is as high as 80%.

Only 16 Pharma Labs are responsible for 90% of sales in this segment and, on average, the percentage of sales on this product category varies between 12% and 35% of total revenue. Patent expirations and technology transfer agreements have spurred the development of domestic production.

Access to medications has been improved with the implementation of the program known as "*Farmácia Popular*" ("Popular Pharmacy"). Since 2011, it has distributed medication for free or at 90% discount to needy people in four thousand cities. The government has spent US$ 4.6 billion with this program.

Growth in the number of people with private health insurance and dental plans has been strong in recent years. Currently there are some 72 million people covered by private health insurance and 21 million of them have some form of dental plan. There are some 1,445 health insurance providers including medical and dental plans. The most recent statistics available indicate total segment revenues of around US$40 billion. Eighty per cent of the plans are corporate, sponsored by the employers.

Recently enacted Law 13.097 allows direct or indirect participation of foreign investors in ownership of health care enterprises. New investments in private hospitals and other related areas in the health market are expected to increase. Two years ago, in 2013, a very large health plan operator Amil was acquired by United Health.

In 2012, CVS acquired Onofre, the eighth largest pharmacy chain in Brazil and is currently analyzing acquisition of the second largest chain DPSP for US$ 2.2 billion.

There are sixty eight thousand pharmacies and drug stores operating in Brazil. Revenues of the largest chains grew 15% in 2014 according to the Brazilian Association of Pharmacies and Drugstore Chains. IMS Health predicts that Brazil will go from tenth to fourth in the global pharmaceutical market by 2018. USA, China and Japan remain top on the list. Those results are consequences of the aging population, low level of unemployment and income growth. Specialists say that this industry will tend to maintain its double-digit growth over the next five years.

Thirty four per cent of total drugstore sales come from cosmetics with women being the main buyers. Today they represent 52% of Brazilian population and most of them are employed and have purchasing power.

The "Popular Pharmacy Program" supported by the Federal Government and generic drugs helped drive the growth of Pharmacies and Drug Stores.

The number of mergers and acquisitions also increased. This kind of business demands economies of scale.

Today, the health care industry accounts for 10.2% of Brazilian GNP with a consistent double-digit annual growth over the past several years.

The eyewear industry is growing in a fast pace and the aging population, income increase and price reduction tend to ensure maintenance of this double-digit growth. The potential market is estimated to be sixty million people who need eyeglasses. The Italian company Luxottica and the French Essilor are taking advantage of this 25% market growth. Forty per cent of this market is based on prescription and sixty per cent are sunglasses.

Tourism Industry

Brazil has a unique opportunity to capture a great share of global tourism. Today, it is ranked sixth by the WTTC in global tourism market. This industry represents only 3.5% of the GNP, below the Latin American average of 4.1 percent. Direct revenues generated are US$ 77.6 billion although it is estimated to add some US$ 205.6 billion to the whole value chain.

Since 2010, the inflow of international tourists has grown 13% and reached 6.4 million people in 2014. Events like the 2014 World Cup and the 2016 Olympics in Rio de Janeiro provide the country visibility and media coverage. These events certainly have brought more investments in the entertainment and hotel industries to mention a few. Most of the tourists coming to Brazil are from Argentina, United States and Chile.

Hotel industry performance has been positive overall, although occupancy rates have dropped due to slower economic growth in 2015.

For some cities like São Paulo where hotels are supported mainly by business traveler volume, occupancy rate levels have remained high during the workweek.

Due to continuous growth of consumer demand, there was an upward pressure on the prices of airline tickets, meals, hotel accommodations as well as entertainment. Rio de Janeiro, considered to be primarily a tourist destination, is viewed today as one of the most expensive in world. As a result, there was a reduction in the number of tourists except during the 2014 World Cup.

The growth in hotel room availability was spurred by the two huge mega-events, and stronger domestic tourism generated by the growing middle class demand. The new development cycle in several regions has led to new hotel openings and stronger performance of existing hotels in these areas. The country's economy has diversified and new areas have been growing. As a result, there are opportunities for new hotels outside of the state capitals and larger cities.

There are 9,681 hotels including the total number of hotels and condo-hotels affiliated with national and international chains that offer some 464,000 rooms in different categories. The main segments of hotel demand in Brazil are: business, leisure and groups. Historically, the business segment brings the highest revenue and demands the middle and high hotel categories.

A total private investment of US$ 4.5 billion is planned for 422 new hotels through 2016. This represents 70,531 new rooms and thirty three thousand direct jobs. In 2014, 164 new hotels were opened for the World Cup held in Brazil. Most of the new hotels will be located in the Southeast Region (59%), followed by the Northeast, South, Central West and North in line with the GNP distribution.

It is important to highlight that most of these new hotel rooms will be in the economic or low cost category (51%) and only 14% can be classified as superior or resort-type. The midscale category will be roughly one-third of the total.

Technological progress

New technologies have helped to increase efficiency in distribution and sales automation. Technological progress came to Brazil and caused disruptions in the banking industries identifying new latent markets.

Banks and financial companies began to deploy sales personnel focused on direct sales using mobile technology for payment. This low-cost innovation and disruptive business model has leveraged retailers who do not have bank accounts. They have been able to sell, using their smartphones equipped with NFC technology (Near Field

Communication) and their sales are credited to a pre-paid card. They have been able to create new markets with new value propositions, offering high technology at low cost to customers.

Business models are essential to convert new technologies into commercial business. Value is necessary to have a new business model to link ideas and technologies to commercial outcomes (Sako, 2012).

Approximately 55 million Brazilians do not have their own bank accounts, representing 26.1% of the population. In 2013, this group spent US$330 billion or 15% of the GNP. On the other hand, 77% of the population already has credit cards, which led many technology information companies to develop mobile payment solutions. AKatus, iZettle, Cielo, Redecard, NTT Data Brasil, Pagpop, Pagtel are some of the players vying for a significant share of this promising market. As one third of the Brazilians already have smartphones, this may be a key factor to stimulate expansion of direct sales and e-commerce. Independent resellers who do not have bank accounts can download an iZettle solution from the Apple store or Google Play to credit their sales on their own pre-paid cards. A commission is charged on each transaction.

Credit cards – As John Elkis, an executive from First Data, the largest credit card processing company, has already said, "Brazil will become very soon the second largest world market for credit card users, behind the United States". That shows the potential market for a young public, willing to deal with new technology in a growing economy. Today, two players dominate the Brazilian market: Cielo and Redecard. New business opportunities are emerging from small- and medium-sized companies and there is a strong demand for mobile solutions for taxis, sales personnel and other kinds of business. To attract more customers credit card companies are offering value added services like lottery prizes or mileage programs, using partnerships.

As most of the suppliers are located in the Southeast Region, eighteen state governments in the North, Northeast and Central West Regions demanded changes in tax law applicable to internet and telemarketing sales. They want to receive the credit for a percentage of the total sales tax, which is currently fully retained in the state where the sale occurs. For some specialists this will be a difficult battle, which will probably wind up raising the cost to the final consumer. Concerning direct sales where taxation is more difficult to control, most of the items usually sold through this channel are taxed at the manufacturer, using the substitute tax system known as *substituição tributária.* Under this system, the first taxpayer, usually the manufacturer withholds all taxes due along the value chain.

Business Model

As Casadesus-Masanell and Ricart (2010) said*: "... every organization has some business model ..., not every organization has a strategy ..."*
There is no agreement on business model descriptions and there are different views on the subject. Among scholars of business models there are some common opinions and they view the business model as a new emerging unit of analysis; as a holistic approach to explaining how companies "do business"; and business models seek to explain how value is created, not just how it is captured (Zott et al.,2011).
Many of the articles explore the connections between the choice of a business model and competitive advantage (Baden-Fuller and Mangematin, 2013).
Companies, which combine entrepreneurship and competitive strategies, are likely to be more able to identify potential opportunities, reallocating resources and developing products and services that meet identified needs.

Dhliwayo (2014) also defends the idea that other areas such as proactivity, risk taking and competitive aggressiveness can build competitive firms.

Business model configuration can be viewed from different dimensions: customer selection, customer engagement, level of innovation, value chain integration, and monetization that is a broader concept of price strategy, partnership development and distribution chain. All of these items can be associated to the mechanisms a company uses to deliver its products or services to the customer.

Different conceptions of business models can act as constraints or opportunities for managerial performance. Innovation in business models has become essential to adapt to new technological, environmental or market challenges.

The fact is that, as the business environment becomes more complex, the potential value of business models also increases. In this context, managers need to gain more knowledge in modeling techniques as an indispensable aid in many business functions (Sako, 2012).

This is the way a company conducts its business in order to best meet the perceived needs of its customers. It seems necessary to identify the set of viable business models managers would find effective for each cluster. New business models can be central to ensure business success.

A well-functioning business model includes several components that fit into the environment conditions. An effective business model proposes customer value; identifies a market segment; defines the structure of the value chain; specifies the revenue generation mechanisms; and also elaborates competitive strategies by which companies obtain and retain competitive advantage.

Exploration of new markets demands entrepreneurial skills. Often it is important to produce systems that do not yet exist, leveraging recent technological developments and creating competitive advantage (Arend, 2013). The concept of new organizational form refers to those characteristics that identify the organization's role as a distinct entity capable of reacting to regional environments and processes of social change.

A strategic renewal may mean that a company has to redefine its relationship with its market, developing new ideas for products and services. Hotels that used to book rooms overnight now offer rooms on a per hour basis a well. In the same way, car rental is now available by the hour in addition to the traditional daily basis. This entrepreneurial way of thinking and doing business has promoted strategic agility, flexibility and continuous innovation as new sources of competitive advantage.

To gather elements for better performance in each region it is important to evaluate the flow of goods and services from firm to consumer. The value chain must include activities to reduce buyer costs or offer product differentiation.

In countries such as Brazil with such a large land area, poor infrastructure, huge population, low per capita income and high potential consumption, shaping the right business model becomes highly relevant.

Today, the average Class C is responsible for 42% of total education expenses in Brazil. Most of them do not have enough income to pay for private schools, but English courses do fit into their budget. In addition, while in the 80's families had an average of 4.4 children, today this number has dropped to 1.7, making it possible to offer a better education to a small student population.

The new social class C has had an increase in income and most (87%) intend to enroll their children in a foreign language course. The number confirms that trend. In 2015, the Brazilian Franchising Association reported a 12% revenue increase in the Education & Training segment over 2014.

To serve this new customer, traditional language courses have developed a new business model, using a new brand for it, known as "micro franchising". This model requires less investment; language schools have from two to four rooms, usually located in low-income areas where students live no more than 3 km away. Monthly cost for students is less than US$ 37. To make this possible, the model requires a simpler infrastructure, reduced number of teachers and timetable. This system operates from Monday to Saturday and the whole course can be taken in two years, half the time of the traditional courses due to its reduced content. CNA, an English course franchise in Brazil is an example of this. Its revenues were R$ 775 million (US$ 287 million) in 2013, almost 30% higher than the year before.

As Parr (1999) considered in his article, merely activating a planned cluster causes a natural growth in a specific geographical area. This situation constructs a favorable environment for growth-minded entrepreneurs. A new phenomenon is taking place in Brazil: spontaneous new cluster development in regional space economy is growing at a faster pace than the national average and an innovative strategy is necessary to address new business opportunities and the variety of regional-problem settings.

A study by the American consulting firm Aberdeen Group shows that seven out of every ten entrepreneurs look for some kind of partnership with other companies. Some of these partners already had some kind of common business. Some of them happened to be suppliers or had some kind of previous experience together. Bryan Ball, vice-president of Aberdeen Group and responsible for the study says that this kind of experience does not simply aim to cut costs but also share knowledge in a new area. It is a pragmatic way of doing new business.

The fear to share confidential information can obstruct competitors from this kind of partnership. BMW, the German carmaker and Japanese competitor Toyota, both players in the luxury automobile market, worked together to innovate. They shared the cost and expertise to develop batteries for electric cars that will be sold in Europe.

It is important to consider infrastructure concentration as one element of the rationale for this strategy. Access to raw materials, energy supply, low-cost labor or a growing domestic market may be some locational advantages. These represent economies of scale in production and sales.

Of course, the presence of a labor force in sufficiently large pools consolidates the advantage of low-cost labor and permits improvements in providing consumer and business services. This fact makes the region in question a more attractive reason for investment (Hoover, 1971, pp. 278±279).

SUBWAY's experience in Brazil shows how important the business model was for its success. The fast food company first arrived in the country in 1994, opened forty stores in the next six years and ended with only two in 2002. The business model demanded large stores and a very high operating cost. In 2005 the model was revised and stores were downsized (32 m^2), working hours made flexible, and more different types of locations defined, including gas stations, supermarkets and university in-store model.

Its first store was located in a three-floor historical building in São Paulo with high fixed costs. In the last five years, with the new business model, SUBWAY opened an average of twelve new stores every month.

The model became more efficient, required initial franchisee investment dropped sharply as well as operating costs, bringing the breakeven point to an attractive level. Today, SUBWAY has 2040 restaurants in Brazil, in 440 different cities, and four hundred new stores are already scheduled to be opened in 2015.

Market trends need to be reviewed periodically. When choosing a strategy, companies make choices among competing alternatives and this may demand a revision of product and service portfolio, production processes and new partnerships. Business flexibility on a continuing basis to gain competitiveness must be allied to a company's capacity to learn from market local conditions.

Strategic competitiveness demands successful formulation and implementation of a value-creation strategy, to guarantee above-average returns and mitigate risks. The fundamental nature of competition in many of the world's industries is changing at an increasingly rapid pace.

Companies who launch products before a strong demand is established can be penalized in the same way as those companies, which arrive after competitors have already established themselves.

In the last ten years, McDonald's sales have been dropping consistently. The bad news is that this will tend to get worse, since the brand is losing its appeal among the millennium generation.

In USA where forty per cent of the 35,000 stores are located, sales dropped in the last twelve months. People between twenty and thirty years, McDonald's target market, are going to the restaurants known as "fast casual ". They are slightly more expensive, but offer better quality food and a more sophisticated environment. Young people are looking for more healthy and fresh food and also have the option to customize their meals for a higher price.

Mc Donald's is trying to use digital communication and offering apps to order and pay on the mobile phone, but other competitors are doing the same and young people nowadays are less loyal to brands.

This reinforces the theory that strategy cannot always remain the same. As Martin Reeves, CEO of Strategy Institute of Boston Consulting Group (BCG), said, the best strategy is to have a number on the sleeve to be able to react to market changes in the same pace.

The company, created almost sixty years ago, has lost its relevance to its consumers. It is facing hyper competition with a new price-quality proposal.

The number of "fast casual" restaurants rose from 9,000 outlets to 21,000, offering better options on their menus.

Adjusting business models to new market demands can be risky and expensive. This is especially true for McDonald's which has a long supply chain and any new item on the menu tends to slow down operations and raise costs.

In order to experiment a new proposal, Mc Café has launched a new concept called "The Corner", in the well-known area on the west side of Sydney, Australia. This new store has a more sophisticated decoration, plants on the balcony, service at the tables, natural ingredients like quinoa and employees wear white aprons.

Mc Donald's has 930 stores in Australia where 1.7 million people are served every day, a significant portion of the country population of 23.5 million people. The public will use this pilot project to measure the acceptance of this new concept. This experiment is the best way to test how deeply the consumer taste has changed keeping the main business responsible for the major part of the cash flow in its original format.

For almost four decades PepsiCo, the second largest drink manufacturer in world, has made money selling soft drinks and greasy snacks with no nutritional attributes. However, consumers have begun to change their habits and obesity is now a major issue.

In 2007, Indra Nooyi, PepsiCo's president, decided to invest most of its advertising budget on healthy crackers. Her intention was to position PepsiCo as a nutritional company conscious of the need for balanced diets by 2020. That proved to be a mistake, at least in the short run, and the consequences of failure were severe. Sales of its famous Pepsi soft drink dropped in the USA market and PepsiCo experienced a significant loss of revenue. Pepsi lost its second position in the ranking to Diet Coke. Stakeholders were not appreciative of that new condition. According to market research, 25% of Americans are strictly healthy in their nutrition; 35% try to be healthy, but are not successful most of the time and the other 45% of American look for taste. The lack of mass media advertising caused the sales drop of Pepsi and that was considered an error. Pepsi was backing the wrong horse.

On the other hand, Coca Cola experienced a drop in its sales in the last eight years and has acquired many other producers of juice, water, tea, and energizers, products, which have been experiencing higher demand. In 2014, Coca Cola was criticized by the amount of its soft drink advertising during the Soccer World Cup in Brazil. These critics said the company should have spent its money acquiring other products in demands and not soft drinks. Coca Cola's explanation was consistent as it explained that 75% of its revenues come from soft drinks and it had to keep its cash cow alive. A wise decision.

The most successful companies seek to find new ways to satisfy current customers and meet the needs of new customers. Unilever has worked on distribution capillarity to leverage its sales in Brazil. Its ice cream sales volume increased 30% in a single year. Per capita consumption is 6.2 liters, low as compared to Europe's per capita figure of 20 liters. This indicates that climate is not the main factor for consumer. Unilever manages the Kibon brand in Brazil, its second largest market right after the U.S. It also brought the American brand Ben&Jerry's to Brazil to reach a market segment willing to pay a premium price. The firm decided to enlarge the product portfolio and enhance distribution creating new packaging for supermarkets, opening kiosks in shopping centers.

Any company's relationship with its customers is enhanced when it delivers them superior value. GE decided to follow this rule offering the consumer a new refrigerator with a coffee machine in it, using Keurig capsules. Whirlpool innovated bringing to the market a new refrigerator with built-in sound equipment. Those new functionalities added to sophistication meet the demand of new customers willing to pay more to have more room in their kitchens.

The purpose of a business-level strategy is to decide whether it is better to perform activities differently or to simply do different things than the competition. That is why companies are committed to understanding current as well as future customer needs.

Operational Innovation

Operational excellence does not mean a high level of performance using existing processes. To innovate means adopting entirely new ways of creating products, filling orders, serving customers or performing any other business activity.

Wal-Mart, Toyota and Dell are examples of companies, which have innovated throughout their history. Their innovations added value to their customers and some helped to reduce cost. Wal-Mart created the cross-docking system, immediately transferring merchandise received from suppliers in the warehouses to the trucks for shipment to stores. The savings from the resulting inventory reduction and optimized operation was transformed in competitive lower prices (Hammer, 2004).

Once products become commodities, businesses need to differentiate their operation to be competitive. Innovation is a continuous process and must be part of the entrepreneurial culture. Sometimes destructive aspects of reorganizing the business must occur to be successful. As most organizations change slowly, the destruction of old processes and methods is relatively obscured (Biggart, 1977). Of course, destructive process must either precede or exist simultaneously with creation. One of the Brazilian groups most well known for their constant structure and methods review is Anheuser-Busch InBev, a Belgian-Brazilian multinational beverage and brewing company headquartered in Belgium and already the world's largest brewer with a 25 per cent global market share before acquiring Miller.

Vertical operation from manufacturing to point-of sale

In an effort to avoid deterioration of profit margins along the channel, some companies have developed their own value chain taking products all the way from the manufacturer to the final consumer. They opened their own stores, used franchising or mixed both models. Besides maintaining a better profit margin along the path, their strategy helped to build consumer loyalty over time to manufacturers' brands.

The idea is to manage manufacturing, distribution and retail enterprises moving product from raw materials to finished goods ready for consumer use. By doing that, manufactures avoid a zero-sum game, in which every retailer's gain is a manufacturer's loss (and vice versa); Of course, that kind of business demands new expertise to manage product assortment at the point of sale, marketing, sales, supply chain and retail infrastructure. Hope, a major lingerie manufacturer, and one of its competitors, *Lupo*, have taken that path. *Havaianas* (sandals), *Boticário* (cosmetics) and *Hering* (fashion apparel) have also adopted the same strategy.

Sharing the Same Points of Sale

Relationships and structure are key sources of competitive advantage. The idea of entrepreneurial networks may minimize risk and transaction costs. Partnerships build on trust and confidence can be valuable.

A business model that has been implemented in Brazil is partnership between different and not competitors companies. As 89% of the cities have less than fifty thousand inhabitants, most businesses are not able to reach the breakeven point in those cities. Considering that, a successful experiment has taken place in Brazil. Three different companies joined forces to open stores in small- and medium-sized cities: *Puket*, a sock franchise; *Imaginarium,* a decoration store and Balonè, a female accessories store, are selling their products together at single stores. They share the same point of sale and split the fixed cost making the business viable at lower sales volumes.

The first store was opened in a small city with less than fifty two thousand inhabitants. In 2012, they opened more than sixty stores. Now they have plans to open 206 new stores by the end of 2016.

They created a new brand called "Love Brands", gathering the different product mix and their target are cities three hundred kilometers away from the large cities with a population of under 200,000. The cost to open each of this kind of store is 60% lower. In addition, it these smaller cities, competition may be non-existent.

Hope, a lingerie industry also decided to increase the number of sales points opening in-store kiosks like the ones usually found in Macy's. The firm focused on that strategy in small cities where they would be unable to reach break-even with their own store.

A new phenomenon in Brazil is taking place: spontaneous development of new clusters in the regional space economy is growing at a faster pace than the national average and an innovative strategy is necessary to face new business opportunities and the diversity of regional-problem settings. The mere activation of a planned pole can cause a natural growth pole in geographical space (Parr, 1999). This situation will build a favorable environment for growth-minded entrepreneurs.

Social Entrepreneurship

For those interested in developing a profitable business and, at the same time, serving the public interest, social entrepreneurship is the right proposal.

Economist and banker Muhammad Yunus first publicized the term "Social Entrepreneurship" in 2006 when he was awarded the Nobel Peace Prize. His bank, Grameen Bank, has the Bangladesh Government as its main stakeholder.

The bank is focused on supplying micro credit to poor people to open their own businesses. Customers have no banking accounts and no credit history profile. Most are women working with handcraft or homemade cheese.

Data from the Word Bank (2008) indicate that more than 3 billion people live on an income of less than US$2.50 a day. This represents over 40% of the world's population.

Brazil also has a large portion of its population at the poverty level.

Many people from rural area have migrated to urban areas, living in slums in very poor conditions. They build their own houses and have limited opportunities to finance their own businesses. Brazilian companies like Natura Ekos have developed partnerships with 19 communities to produce the raw material from its cosmetic plants, an initiative that has benefitted 1714 families. Making money, performing charity or doing the right thing seem to be compatible.

The path blazed by Muhammad Yunus stimulated young entrepreneurs to follow his lead and develop socially responsible and profitable businesses.

Social entrepreneur Marcelo Fukuyama disseminated the concept in Brazil. His Company CDI, originally created as an

NGO funded solely by donations began to make profit and changed its business model. It uses technology to qualify low-income young people.

B-Team is another example. It is represented in Brazil by Natura advisor, Guiherme Leal, and led by Richard Branson, Virgin founder and Jochen Zeitz, chairman of Puma. It proposes business solutions in order to conciliate profit, social and environmental responsibility.

The *Dr. Consulta* ("Dr. Medical Visit") clinic serves the local population in a slum in Southern Brazil. Patients have fifteen different medical specialists available for only R$ 80 (roughly US$ 21.60). Medical exams like blood tests are also available at the same location for only R$ 10 each (US$ 2.70). Today, approximately 5 000 patients are attended monthly. At public health facilities, they were used to waiting three months for these services.

A chain of 300 dental service clinics has annual revenues of U$ 90 million. It is also focused on low-income consumers with limited resources to pay for dental care.

The business model has succeeded. The objective now is to quickly replicate it, on a large scale with lower gross margins but with a large number of customers. Maintaining a low cost business model has proven to be a successful way of doing business in Brazil.

Roughly, US$ 46 billion are dedicated to this market today. In 2010, JP Morgan Bank and the Rockefeller Foundation, one of the more traditional philanthropic institutions in USA projected total outlays in the so-called "impact investment" segment from US$ 400 billion to US$ 1 trillion by 2020. This impact investment has a two-sided purpose: improve social conditions and environmental conditions and guarantee return on investment.

In 2013, 125 institutions invested US$ 10.6 billion in the "impact investment" segment worldwide (GIIN and JP Morgan research).

These new entrepreneurs are pragmatic. Many of them have worked for huge companies developing solid business experience and for them, profit is not a sin. As soon as "impact investments" generate profit, more investors will be attracted. In many cases, returns on investment range from 10% to 35% a year.

Building up a profitable business able to contribute to change where value lies can be a challenge. It is necessary to change the mindset and work toward developing a new solution.

It is necessary to consider new issues, new solutions, new patterns and new paradigms. In fact, the right amount of socially responsible capitalism can be the antidote to uncontrolled capitalism, necessary to transform the world.

Product and Price Strategy

"Price definition is the moment of truth – everything in Marketing comes under focus in the price decision". Raymond Corey – Harvard Business School

New product introductions, if successful, go hand in hand with first-mover competitive advantage. Proactive organizations are inclined to take risks in pursuing opportunities and having the foresight to act to anticipate future demand and shape the environment, a posture aimed at beating the competition.
Novelty-centered business models focus on product market strategies that emphasize differentiation, cost leadership or early market entry to enhance firm performance (Zott and Amit, 2008).

New product development (NPD) is becoming an important competitive advantage in the marketing strategies of current businesses (Liao, 2011). As part of marketing strategy, a company must take into account the price level related to product/market segmentation. Each segment contains a number of customers with a similar set of requirements and desires that make them generally more or less attractive. Market segments can be reached by different marketing-mix aspiration levels and companies often adjust their basic price to accommodate differences in customer characteristics.

Dove, the first soap with moisturizer in Brazil, had the chance to create a new reference price for this kind of product in the market. At the time the soap was launched in the Brazilian market, the leading competing product was LUX soap, sold at one third of Dove's price. The company was able to behave as a monopolist in this market, moving first into the sales channels and making a take-it-or-leave-it offer of its wholesale price to all retailers.

Price has a hedonic function and it is relevant to analyze the relationship between quality signals and price setting (Abrate, Capriello and Fraquelli, 2011).

Sensodyne toothpaste was for many years the only product available for consumers with sensitive teeth. Its price at the point-of-sale was around

R$ 13.00 (US$ 3.51). Colgate identified this market opportunity and launched its own product. Its price strategy was to make this new product available at the supermarkets at half Sensodyne's price (R$ 6.50 or US$ 1.75). Of course, consumers questioned if this product had the same quality of the leader they already knew. If Colgate had sold its toothpaste at R$ 9.50 (US$ 2.57) it would have offered the consumer an advantage and certainly have minimized the suspicion that it might not be as good as the competitor at half the price.

A product position of superior quality implies a premium price in consumers' minds.

Developing a country-level strategy demands a careful analysis of the marketing environment in Brazil, including what is the best way for segmenting and targeting markets, local competition, supply chain management and best pricing strategy.

Another important fact to be considered in price strategy is the concept of "monetization". This is a key part of value capture and involves more than just pricing as it also includes systems determining timings of payments and revenue collection methods (Baden-Fuller and Mangematin, 2013).

A price is incurred in exchange for receiving a bundle of benefits. The right price required to provoke a certain purchase behavior may be associated with a change in product to eliminate barriers to engaging in the exchange. (Thackeray and Brown, 2010)

For some companies it may be necessary to adopt different price policies based on the kind of customers they wish to serve. Using the Telecom industry as an example, companies can target a variety of customers, ranging from single consumers to national governments changing not only their products and services, but also their price modeling. That may represent a challenge for some companies. Some companies neglect the idea that pricing can be a source of competitive advantage and it can play a role in strategic positioning.

Considering budget restriction, telecom companies invested in pre-paid services that account today for 70% of the total mobile lines. There are approximately 270 million mobile lines in the market. The ARPU – Average revenue per user in the pre-paid segment is very low, but companies play with higher gross profit margins. They charge higher rates per minute, lower their business risk and are able to serve low-income consumers.

According to Zeithaml (1988) value is a combination of what a customer wishes (consciously or subconsciously), perceived quality, and the perceived extrinsic (e.g. price and brand name) and intrinsic attributes (e.g. flavor, color and texture) of the offering.

A mission statement should be focused on the market the company is attempting to serve rather than on the specific good or service offered.

The five-dimensional "SBIFT price model" (considering the dimensions: Scope, Base, Influence, Formula and Temporal rights) developed by Iveroth, Westelius et al. (2013) highlighted some important aspects to be considered by companies in their price strategy:

The first is the scope, which refers to the granularity of the offer. In other words, this means pricing the lowest-level individual unit or a complete product package.

The second dimension refers to pricing based on production cost or customer value perception. In Brazil, the cost to produce brown rice is lower than that to produce white rice, but the value perceived by customers makes the brown rice almost fifty per cent more expensive.

The third dimension deals with the extent to which either the seller or the buyer are able to influence selling price. Many years ago, industries responsible for their branded products were the ones who dictated sales prices in the market. That power, however, migrated to the sales channels. These channels grew so large opening their own branches or working with franchised stores that manufacturers depend on them to get to customers.

In some cases, it became even worse for manufacturers because retailers developed their own private labels and some industries became just commodity supplier for retailers.

The fourth dimension of the SBIFT model is related to the formula used to connect price with volume. Companies can define fixed unit prices regardless of volume or work with variable combinations like guaranteed contracting for a certain volume of the offering, and get paid for a fixed amount regardless of whether that quantity is used or not. Once again, the negotiating power between seller and buyer is taken into account.

The fifth and last dimension is related to temporal rights. It focuses on for how long customers have the right to use any given product or service.

This can vary from a single sale where the consumer will not have the right to any enhancements that the seller makes to the product or service, to a perennial offering. The latter is very common in software industry contracts, where, after purchase, companies adhere to a subscription plan that includes upgrades and enhancements made by the seller.

The SBIFT model captures some different and relevant aspects most considered in the price strategy. However, it is important to highlight what must be the central concern when companies attempt to set an appropriate price for their products and services: market adherence to the product and above all, the customer's capacity to pay for it. Working on payment terms, financing possibilities or changes in unit of sale, pricing strategy can become a road for business success.

WALMART's positioning of "everyday low price" is a good example of that. It developed its private labels for food products like ice cream, organic eggs from unconfined hens, cookies and more than 750 items, including breakfast cereal, cookies, yogurt, laundry detergent, and paper towels. For consumable pharmacy and health and beauty items, such as shaving cream, skin lotion, over-the-counter medications, and pregnancy tests the Equate brand was used, an example of the strength of WALMART's private label store brand. WALMART manages five of the top 10 "likely to purchase" private label brands.

Supermarket chain Carrefour created its own private label in 1976 and brought it to Brazil in 1989. Today the firm sells more than 14,000 products under eleven different private brands. They represent forty percent of total sales in Brazil (Nielsen).

Manufacturers often have only general information about whole market and demographic patterns. However, retailers have point-of-sale data and detailed knowledge of regional consumer behavior. The dominant retailers such as chain supermarkets became more powerful commanding a large market share in the retail market (Yan, Myers and Wang, 2012).

Mattel, the toy company, would hardly sell their products if WALMART and TOYS "R" US did not agree to include the products in their assortment. Today, industries depend on retailers to sell and price strategy must fit their profitability target.

Opportunities in Brazil are rapidly moving beyond the largest cities, often the focus of many companies. In order to attend this new demand it is necessary to develop regionally: product innovation, price, logistics and communication strategy.

In the B2B (business to business) model the profit margin of the retailer guaranteed by the manufacturer can be more relevant than the final price of the product at point-of-sale. Many years ago, PROCTER & GAMBLE decided to print the suggested sale price on a laundry soap package expecting to gain market share. One of its important retailers, 7-ELEVEN, Inc. the world's largest convenience store chain with close to 53,000 stores in 16 countries, more than 10,350 of which in North America, refused to sell this product in their stores. The printed price did not meet the firm's profit margin expectations. Of course, P&G had to review this price policy. Companies, which depend on resellers, must be aware of the importance of channel profitability.

Airlines and Insurance brokerage companies used to depend on their agents and consequently their interest in commissions to reach final consumers. E-commerce has helped them to minimize that dependence.

In Brazil, different social classes may represent different and profitable business opportunities. The dominant "C" class, the middle class, is the largest with approximately one hundred and ten million people with an average family income of US$ 20,800. In recent years, Class C consumption has been driven by financing and tax incentives that have been strongly stimulated by governmental banks.

The right price needed to generate a specific purchasing behavior may be associated with a change in the product to eliminate the barriers to engaging in the exchange (Thackeray and Brown, 2010). In fact, it is the customer who truly determines price (Shaw, 1992).

A good example of that is DANONE's price strategy adopted in the country's Northeast region where most of the population has an income level below the already-low national average. The way the organization set its prices changed customer behavior and had a long-lasting impact on customer relationships.

The company's strategy allowed DANONE to win many new consumers not able to pay for a full tray of yogurt and to make more profit. Instead of selling the tray with six yogurts for R$ 4.80 (US$ 1.30), DANONE offered only single units for R$ 0.90 each (US$ 0.24).

1 tray = R$ 4,80 **1 unit = R$ 0,90**

The specific content of this strategy is the commitment to serve the unique needs of this market segment, and the firm's competitive position within its business environment. The company not only made more profit; it did so in a way to offer benefit for its potential consumers. It also enhanced the consumer's perceived value for that particular purchase.

Another successful price strategy was used by Cialis to face the leadership of Viagra, the first sexual stimulant sold in Brazilian market. Viagra used to be sold in a package with four units and many users reported some collateral effects when taken after alcohol consumption. Applying an innovated marketing strategy, Cialis offered its product in a single unit package, developed a training program for retailers to explain that the product would be effective for 36 hours, and offered sellers a sales incentive program. Cialis became a market leader in few months. Although its sales price was reduced, gross margin was increased.

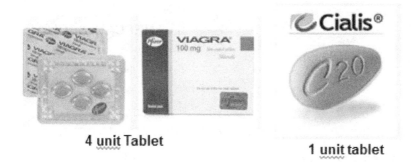

4 unit Tablet

1 unit tablet

Zeng (2103) discussed the theory of how the consumer experience affects the retailer's optimal pricing strategy and profit. In this case, as new customers are anxious to buy the product for the first time, and they are more likely to pay a premium, price analysis based on different packages does not occur. Besides that, after observing prices for purchases in both packages, purchase budgets restricted by low income also influence this situation.

Following the same strategy of sales-oriented pricing, NESTLE changed packaging of certain products like powdered chocolate and oatmeal, from tin cans to sachets, in smaller quantities, to be able to lower prices and increase its market share in the region.

 **NESCAU CAN**    **NESCAU SACHET**

Brand extension strategies enhance brand positioning, awareness and increase probability of trial by consumers by diminishing new product risk for consumers (Taylor and Bearden, 2002).

COCA-COLA also launched two new package forms: a returnable glass bottle which can be reused at least twenty five times thus considerably reducing final product price for the family home market; and a new small 250 ml can that can be sold for R$ 1.00 (equivalent to US$ 0.27). This latter option is for consumers looking for an inexpensive and fast snack option. When purchased together with a snack item, total final price remains below US$ 0.55. These new package options led to a 15% increase in revenues and were distributed in more than 190,000 points of sale.

Pricing is vital when strategies are developed. The links between the strategy, price modeling and the competitive arena are rather straightforward (Iveroth, Westelius et al., 2013). COCA-COLA is facing a decrease in soft drink sales over the last eight years due to competition from juices, mineral water, tea and low-price locally produced soft drinks known as *"tubaínas"*.

In a consumer market where there are different segments with high and low income, it is relevant to consider price elasticity of demand separately by segment. For wealthy consumers, a lower price does not mean an increase in consumption, under the standard economic assumption that customers behave rationally. When companies deal with low-income segments, a business model concerning pricing tactics is essential to generate demand for the product. Promotional strategy or lowering the price level based on package size can be very effective for low-income customers.

Demand sets the ceiling for pricing decisions; in other words, what the market will bear. In this scenario, it is relevant to consider information technology (IT) as an important tool to manage pricing practices in a multifaceted model. The pricing model may differ by consumer segment or even by the level of competition in each region. Retailers usually adopt that regional pricing strategy, making more profit where there is no competition. Changes in market conditions may force companies to continuously rethink their pricing models.

IT resources and the Internet have provided tools to assist companies in their pricing strategies through increased information availability to react to market changes and improve reach and interactivity between them and market channels. As a result, IT has opened up the opportunity for companies to adopt a vast array of price strategies such as premium versions, bundles and regional approaches.

Channel coordination of price and non-price decision variables are not always controlled by manufacturers. Quantity discounts can be used for that purpose, but coordination is not always in the interest of manufacturers when they sell to independent retailers that compete among themselves for customers.

Price-setting strategy is relevant because of what it means to seller revenues and represents the primary source of profits. In addition, price plays two roles in the evaluation of product alternatives by the consumer: as a measure of sacrifice and as an information cue. In the broadest sense, price assures product positioning in the consumer's' mind, as a way to infer the product's quality and status.

The classical analysis-explaining price in terms of supply and demand still remains essentially the most acceptable explanation of the phenomena of price determination. Demand sets the ceiling for pricing decisions, in other words, what the market will bear.

The relationship between a company's corporate strategy and its internal administrative structure can be related to some of them outperforming others. Depending on its structure, a company may more quickly tailor its offerings and react to customer preferences. Technology has also enabled companies to change fundamentally the ways they organize and transact across the organization and market.

The business model works as a source of value and the organization's structure may affect the pattern of transactions between the company and external stakeholders.

Distribution and Logistics Strategy

Brazil has tremendous infrastructure problems. With a huge territory, it is the world's fifth largest country and represents 47% of South America's landmass. Freight transportation cost is a major issue. Only 16% of the roads are paved. Historically, freight represents 25% of product cost. In some regions like the North, this percentage can be as high as

39.5%. Ship transportation is also limited and internal waterways account for only 13% of all cargo shipped.

Due to this poor transportation infrastructure, it is a challenge to serve the whole market from South to North.

Federal and State governments intend to leverage investments motivating the partnership between public and private investments for the development of multimodal transportation, using coastal shipping, which has been growing at a double digit rate over the last five years, highway and rail transportation. This can mean a 20-30% savings on transportation costs especially for commodity items. It represents 11.5% of the GNP. Transportation of grains is the most demanding considering that it requires a very large number of trucks to ship the whole production.

The National Integrated Logistics Plan (PNLI), a 20-year long-term government plan, helps to identify short- and long-term needs, considering the volume of production by region, taking into account its origin and destination and helping to develop economic feasibility for each individual project. Along with these investments, truck, ship and railroad industries will become important suppliers to support this strategy.

Distribution involves the processes that facilitate successful commercial transactions. The functions of distribution can be very complex and they involve information dissemination, physical distribution, promotion, contact and matching needs that fulfill completed transactions including risk taking and financing (Day, Ward, Choi and Zhao, 2011).

Considering the country's huge territorial extension and infrastructure problems, companies must define their best logistics system. Direct Shipping strategy which is an easy-to-implement distribution strategy frequently used in industrial distribution system or, in cases where direct shipping strategy has proven to be ineffective, a more general Fixed Partition Policy (FPP) combining direct shipping strategy and multiple-stop shipping can be used (Li, Chen and Chu, 2010). Distribution of a product from manufacturers to multiple retailers is usually realized through warehouses using a fleet of vehicles. A cost- benefit analysis is necessary based on performance evaluation of the inventory routing problem and the delivery frequency constraint.

The effectiveness of an FPP depends on the total demand rate of the retailers in each partition (each retailer set) and their degree of proximity. Operating with multiple and integrated warehouses for inventory restocking and strategically located in regions with sales concentration can, in the long-run, minimize average total transportation and inventory costs of the system. This performance evaluation must be related to the economic lot size of the retailers, vehicle capacity, and distance from the warehouse to retailer and the fixed transportation cost in firm's cost structure.

CACAU SHOW is a very large chocolate store chain in Brazil. It has approximately 1900 stores spread all over the country. Its logistics can be complex considering that it launches a set of new products every two weeks and they are perishable. That issue becomes more critical during the Easter period when franchisees need to define what level of inventory they should carry for the period. In this case, the less frequent and effective the distribution system, the more risk adverse franchisees will become, buy, and stock less even though they may be running the risk of losing sales.

A company's supply chain management requires coordination and integration of all activities performed by members of the process, from source to point of consumption. In addition, most importantly, it must be completely customer driven. In Brazil, in the Southeast and South regions, five supermarket chains account for 82% of all food and beverage distribution. In the other regions like Central West, North and Northeast there are over 200,000 small- and medium-sized supermarkets. This kind of situation demands intensive commercial and logistics capillarity.

Thus, any company interested in serving such demanding markets, will need either have their own local distribution centers or develop channel partnerships to serve customers and create a competitive advantage.

Some routes in the North Region can represent major challenges:

If they cooperate, retailers, wholesalers, manufactures and suppliers will be able to increase inventory turnover, improve customer service and reduce costs of the marketing channel. Those specific regions demand that companies have a more competitive spatial structure to meet the local demand (Parr, 1978).

NESTLE has wisely worked to develop alliances with local entrepreneurs to build local distribution centers with strict storage and shipment criteria. Product portfolios have been differentiated by the type of sales channel and distribution centers located in strategic cities. Each DAN- Authorized Nestlé Distributor has a pre-defined geographic area to cover, thus avoiding competition among distributors.

In addition, Nestle has signed an agreement to serve 80,000 people who live along the banks of the Amazon River. A floating store developed on a boat is the way to achieve that objective.

Two huge banks, CEF – Caixa Econômica Federal, government-owned and the second largest private bank Bradesco took the same approach to attract customers living along the river.

Not every company has found the best way to manage the challenges of a huge country like Brazil with so many regional cultures. CENCOSUD, a Chilean supermarket chain, spread around the country and ranked fourth in sales in Brazil is having trouble trying to manage stores in the South, Central and North regions in the same way using a centralized model. It attempted to centralize its purchasing department, logistics, promotion decisions and operating costs rose. The central office was not able to promptly meet local demands. Out-of-stock or overstocked conditions began occurring frequently. This model caused losses for the business.

As Philip Kotler called "The third basis for positioning" strategy (1996), that refers to segmenting customers who are accessible in different ways. Many companies in Brazil have made use of this strategy. While many multinational companies had no interest in customers in the North and Northeast regions, local industries developed large and profitable businesses. Their strategy was to produce private brands and sell locally in small rather than large cities, and to customers spread out geographically instead of those concentrated in a single region. They made use of local human resources and specific designed marketing, logistics and sale service arrangements to meet local needs.

In response to highly volatile and uncertain environments, many companies have implemented distribution flexibility driven by market dynamism (Yu, Song and Cadeaux, 2012) Product life cycles have become shorter and existing routines and procedures may be ineffective.

The contemporary business environment forces many distribution companies to make adaptations in channel relationships, reviewing the process and structure.

In a country where transportation can represent as much as thirty per cent of final product cost, it is important to emphasize the use of the most efficient transportation mode to reduce the number and volume of trips. Any choice of flexible distribution strategy must take into account the business environment and supply chain. Partners share the responsibility to respond rapidly to customer demand at each link in the chain.

In this context, a distributor should be able to offer either broad geographical distribution or intensive coverage in a specific area to rapidly and effectively adjust inventory levels, package sizes, provide storage facilities and physical transportation to respond quickly and timely to customer service needs.

Along the value chain, it is vital to develop relationship management processes between partners through integrative capabilities. Each company must systematically balance or combine different dimensions under varying conditions.

Hilletofth, Hilmola and Claesson (2011) have focused their study on an in-transit distribution strategy that is to transform the transportation pipeline into a mobile inventory storage location, and actively dispatch goods to destinations, where there is a predicted demand before any customer orders are actually received.

The use of this strategy is supported by current trade flows: emerging market trade has increased considerably.

A decentralized distribution strategy often leads to shorter lead-time and higher flexibility, while the main disadvantage is that products may have to be stored at several places, which corresponds to significantly higher warehousing costs, although it could still be interesting from a cost and tied-up capital point of view.

In-transit distribution strategy can be used as a complement in centralized/decentralized distribution structures. This means that products or goods that are being transported are used as mobile inventory. Companies can dispatch goods to a destination based on a predicted demand, before any customer order is received. This can increase inventory turnover, but it is also important that the costs for this intermediate storage are not excessively high and handling is relatively simple.

There is no one single distribution solution for all kinds of products and markets and there are clear differences among Brazil's different regions.

Regardless of the distribution flexibility strategy chosen to contribute to fit local environment conditions, supply chain partners must share the responsibility to respond rapidly to customer demand at each link of the chain.

Companies must ally the ability to provide widespread or intensive distribution coverage to adjust inventory quickly and effectively, packaging, warehousing, and transportation of physical to responding to customer needs for service, delivery time, and price.

An enterprise resource planning system able to support the process and working closely with customers are prerequisites. This strategy also requires low demand variations and distribution lead times.

Consider for example, MC DONALD's need to receive lettuce every day. As a perishable item, considering that, it has more than 1700 stores and the fact it has recently opened new stores which can be more than two thousand kilometers from the producer, an in-transit distribution strategy may be plausible. This need is also a problem for those more than four hundred thousand fast food stores in Brazil and, according to the British consulting firm Mintel this number may increase 47% by 2018.

Some publishers have adopted an in-transit distribution system, visiting each of the book stores with their vehicles loaded with the most marketable items and best sellers.

Some manufacturers have also adopted the mobile shop concept. As most cities in Brazil are not large enough to have an onsite store, consumers may be served by periodic visits of those trucks converted into mobile stores.

In recent years, as per capita income in the Northeast increased at an average rate of 7.3% a year, double the national average and demand arose for new products; new distribution centers have been built to minimize delivery time to retailers and final consumers of direct sales and e-commerce. They also helped small regional distributors, demanding from them lower inventory and working capital investment.

Partnership is also a good strategy in this filed. SOUZA CRUZ, a British American Tobacco, the tobacco leader in Brazil and also considered to be a benchmark in distribution, has become responsible for Procter & Gamble, Red Bull and BIC's logistics. It distributes consumer products like pens, lighters and razors for these companies. SOUZA CRUZ trucks take those products to 465,000 sales points. In 2011, the volume of BIC products sold by SOUZA CRUZ increased by 52% over 2010 volume. BIC's inventory level dropped from fifty to twenty days and operational costs went down. Red Bull reported a 30% sales increase after this partnership was established.

The distribution deal has been renewed every two years in the last eight years.

Franchising

The Franchising business model has been growing in Brazil over the last twenty-five years. It preaches a new culture of multiplier management, a promising trend in Brazil. According to the World Franchise Council, Brazil has the third largest franchising business, after China and South Korea. More than 480 different brands were presented in the 23rd edition of ABF Franchising Expo in Brazil, in 2014. It represents 2.3% of Brazil's GNP, compared to USA where it accounts for 3.8%. Revenue has consistently increased over the last ten years and reached R$ 134 billion (US$ 44 billion) in 2015.

Approximately 3,073 brands are making use of franchising operation in Brazil and they manage 138, 343 stores and one million employees.

Some local companies have already found their way to internationalization. More than one hundred Brazilian chains have international operations with presence in fifty countries. Some banks offer special guaranteed funding for the franchises at favorable interest rates. In 2015, twenty Brazilian brands started operation overseas totalizing 134 retail chains.

For over a decade, franchising outperformed the Brazilian GNP in terms of growth. In fact, franchise revenues have grown at an average annual rate of seventeen per cent over the last five years while the Gross National Product increased less than five per cent a year over the same period.

Many international brands have adopted the franchising business model to expand their businesses in Brazil. Burger King, Mc Donald's, Subway, Starbucks, KFC, Havanna, the biggest *alfajor* producer from Argentina. Applebees, Kiel's from L'Oreal, and Mac cosmetics are some successful examples operating in Brazil. The franchise business model can be a good option for foreign investors. It minimizes the risk of unknown regional differences as it adds partners with local business expertise to the model.

The strategy of franchising has been adopted by many companies as a way of reaching different and remote areas in the country and expands the supply chain. This business model has fulfilled the need to take products, services and brands to all corners of the country.

Its tendency of expansion is leveraged by the single and simplified legislation that favors the franchisee and franchisor in most cases. Federal Law No. 8,955, enacted in 1994, establishes the requirements for the preparation and presentation of a Franchise Offer Circular to potential franchisee candidates whenever franchisors are interested in using a system of free enterprise (Article 3). The rise of social classes C and D that today represent two thirds of the population and millions of people, the end of high inflation, the increase in the number of formal jobs and many social programs are important drivers to the franchising business model to address the new consumer profile. Franchising is the quickest way to expand a business brand in the market, with low investment. Approximately 92% of the companies in Brazil have less than ten employees and most of them operate in the retail or service segment.

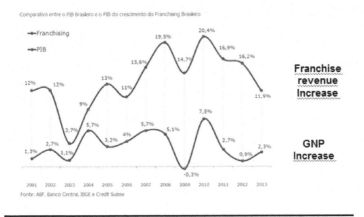

Comparativo entre o PIB Brasileiro e o PIB do crescimento do Franchising Brasileiro

→ Franchising
→ PIB

Franchise revenue Increase

GNP Increase

2001 2002 2003 2004 2005 2006 2007 2008 2009 2010 2011 2012 2013
Fonte: ABF, Banco Central, IBGE e Credit Suisse

Figure: Franchise revenue X GNP increase

Source: ABF, Banco Central, IBGE and Credit Suisse

They manage 138, 343 points of sale or branches around the country. Most of them (52.6%) are located in São Paulo, the country's largest city. (Source: http://www.portaldofranchising.com.br).

Another important factor is related to the increasing population migration in this huge country. In 2013, thirty nine per cent of Brazilians were living in different places from where they were born. The growth of the franchising business in the countryside shows the maturity of the sector that promotes a complete reform of the retailing, introducing new management processes, technologies and generation of new jobs to former urban centers professionals. Most of them started operation in small cities with less than fifty inhabits. They are located in 40% of the municipalities.

The franchising model has been adapted to some new sectors like hospitals, hotels, restaurants, general services and tourism. This marriage between entrepreneurship and franchising is a consequence of the Brazilian profile: A study by Endeavor indicates that 76% of Brazilians intend to become entrepreneurs. For newcomers to the business world, the franchising system lower risks, supporting them with business plan, market research, training program and control over supplier negotiation. The best commercial practices and performance standards are applied in smaller towns to where Brazilians are currently migrating.

On the other hand, taxes applied to franchising business require a more careful analysis.

The Brazilian Federal Constitution (1988) conferred the power to levy taxes to States, the Federal District and Municipalities, assuming the existence of wealth in the form of income, property and consumption. In the franchise relationship, taxable wealth consists of the remuneration owed by the franchisee to the franchisor. This payment can be made in Brazil related to domestic operations, from Brazil to abroad when related to international import operations. In each case, the way taxes are charged will vary.

Taxes charged on domestic operations on franchisor remuneration include: Municipal Service Tax (ISS), Contribution to the Social Integration Program (PIS), the Contribution to Finance Social Security (COFINS), Corporate Income Tax (IRPJ) and Social Contribution on Net Earnings (CSLL).

When the franchisor has no domicile in Brazil and the franchisee is a Brazilian Company, remuneration is subjected to the following taxes: Income Tax Withheld at Source (IRRF), Contribution on Intervention in the Economic Domain (CIDE), PIS-Import, COFINS-Import, ISS and the Tax on Financial Operations (IOF).

When the international capital flow is reversed meaning that the franchisor is a Brazilian Company and the franchisee has no domicile in Brazil, only corporate taxes are due (IRPJ and CSLL), as this income is not subject to the PIS and COFINS and exempt from having to pay the Municipal ISS tax.

There is a special tax regime that encompasses the charging and collection of IRPJ, CSLL, and also includes IPI (Industrial Products Tax), Cofins, PIS, the Employer's

Contribution Pension –CPP, ICMS (State Value Added Tax) and ISS. It is called *Simples Nacional*. This regime is designed specifically for businesses with gross annual revenues of up to R$ 3.6 million or approximately US$ 1 million. There are some other requirements to be able to qualify for this benefit such as: the company is not allowed to have a participating partner domiciled abroad in its capital stock nor any outstanding debts with the Brazilian Social Security Administration (INSS) or Federal, State or Municipal Treasuries.

In a scenario where taxation can have many nuances, tax planning is welcome to Investors. It helps taxpayers obtain savings legally by adopting a business model with the lowest tax impact on revenues.

Direct Sales

The direct sales model allows companies to reach places where they would not be profitable using any other business model.

Brazil is the fifth largest direct sales market in world, with total revenue of US$ 13 billion in 2014 with a 3-Year CAGR in Constant 2014 USD (2011-14) of 6.7%. It represents nine per cent of total world volume (The World Federation of Direct Selling Associations-WFDSA) and 0.75% of Brazil's GNP. Approximately 12 million people are directly involved in this business, more than the population of Uruguay, and they make a profit of more than US$ 5 billion a year. Most of those involved in this business are women (75%) and 25% are men, working for the largest direct sales companies in world like AMWAY, TUPPERWARE, AVON, MARY KAY, BELCORP, NATURA, HERBALIFE and many others.

Figure 8: Global Direct Selling

Source: http://www.wfdsa.org/files/pdf/global-stats/sales-report-2014.pdf

This growth of direct sales can be explained from the point of view of benefits to the independent representatives: this kind of job offer flexible work schedules, improvement in socioeconomic conditions and direct sales can be a key source of family income.

Additionally, the fact that this kind of sale is very personal, trusting the independent sales representative becomes very relevant, making product sales practically recommendations in this kind of business. For some retail companies, this sale channel complements their market capillarity, especially in those cities where a physically store would not be able to reach breakeven. BOTICARIO, a very large retail chain with 3,760 cosmetic stores, developed this channel in parallel and store managers are responsible for indicating three thousand independent sales representatives. Today 40% of total cosmetic products sales are made door to door.

In this scenario, e-commerce has become an ally. Some companies have promoted the development of online stores for their independent sales representatives. All they have to do is to promote them among their customers. Customers can buy on credit and receive products at home within 48 hours. Sales reps automatically get their sales commissions. Electronic catalogues are available to all reps and are easily updated. Social networks are also contributing to this kind of business. Nowadays, people are multi-channel consumers and the X and Y generations were born in a digital era.

The portfolio ranges from cosmetics and personal care (35%) to health products (25%), consumer goods (14%), clothing and accessories (9%) and many other items such as books, lingerie, computers, stationary, financial services, food and beverages. This sale channel has helped consolidate the national per capita consumption of perfume, which is now the highest in world (US$ 249) vs. a world average of US$ 60.40. Beauty products are responsible for 90% of total revenue.

NESTLE, the Swiss company, has also managed this kind of channel. Initially targeting small communities the company created a program with fifteen thousand independent sales representatives supplying 800 different products to 291 exclusive micro-distributors, who serve 720,000 residences and 2.4 million people. Its second step was to create a floating store (boat) that sails along the Amazon River serving 1.5 million people living in twenty-seven different riverside cities. Together, these programs reach 3.9 million consumers and are considered as great successes.

Other companies have been increasing their market shares using the direct sale channel to sell mattresses, pillows, sheets, pans and home appliances all focused on lower class consumers living far from the big cities.

AVON has 1.5 million independent sales representatives, NATURA has1.3 million and MARY KAY has 300 thousand working for them.

VIVO, a Telecom company, adopted this channel to sell telephone lines, satellite TV, and mobile internet for those consumers who do not feel comfortable going to a store.

The industrial market is also using this channel. TOTVS, a multinational software company operating in 23 countries, has focused on small businesses in Brazil that represents 85% of all companies (some ten million enterprises). Doctors' offices, bakeries, coffee shops, law offices, hair dressers are their target market for simple technological solutions ranging from inventory control to issuing invoices and tax books.

Local and unique solutions are demanded in business strategy and can make the difference in the competition game. In a huge country like Brazil, it is relevant to explore multiple sales channels that offer a better capillarity.

In terms of logistics, cosmetics suppliers have invested in local distribution centers to be able to serve sixty million households in Brazil's five regions. To avoid difficulty with urban mobility and ensure on-time delivery, bicycles and electric vehicles are being used.

This business is based on the number of representatives and the amount of bonus and prizes distributed among them. Mary Kay, for example, intends to reward its best reps in 2015 with more than 700 automobiles such as Mercedes and BMWs at a cost of R$ 270 million (US$ 73 million).

E-commerce

E-commerce is a relatively new way of doing business. This concept entered the business vocabulary in the 1970s; however, it began to gain prominence at the end of the 20[Th] century with the development of a digital world. The widespread use of personal computers, proliferation of the internet, as well as the development of on-line payment security systems have been the main drivers for e-commerce development.

In today's world, e-commerce has become an important alternative sales channel for virtually all retailers. However, it can mean different things to different people. Zwass (1996), for example, defines e-commerce as "the sharing of business information, maintaining business relationships and conducting business transactions by means of telecommunications networks". Others (Applegate, 1999, Fellenstein and Wood, 2000) also support this view and consider e-commerce to include several processes inside and outside organizations in addition to purchasing and selling activities.

E-commerce is considered in its most common and popularized use known as B-to-C (business to consumer). According to (Molla & Licker: E-Commerce Systems Success, 2001) in this type of e-commerce, organizations offer their products and services and generate revenue from the actual sale of those products and services to their customers.

The internet and e-commerce are affecting distribution management strategies and consumer behavior in new ways, which need to be examined more closely. Small enterprises can now reach niche markets, which, until the advent of the internet, were not cost effective to serve. The impact of internet-based distribution on the demand curve has implications for both consumers and strategists (Day, Ward, Choi and Zhao, 2011).

Along with this expansion, discussion of which e-commerce business model is more profitable is very common. Does the model vary according to the product assortment or need to be adapted based on the target market and the region where it is located?

The world has witnessed the US$ 21.8 billion Alibaba IPO, a record for the U.S., reaching values higher than Facebook Inc. and Amazon.com Inc.

On the other hand, investors have been discussing for how long this kind of business will be able to consistently generate profit. Its revenues come from advertising and sales commissions. Alibaba's CEO, Mr. Jack Ma, classified the business not as an e-commerce, but as a virtual shopping center. In fact, it does not sell its own products. This business model has provided Alibaba with a higher operating margin (43.4%) than eBay Inc. (18%), Google Inc., (27%) and Amazon, which registered a negative operating margin of 0.1% over the same period.

Alibaba's business model is an interesting case for discussion. Its operation alters the traditional value chain model to serve customers and provide service as no physical product moves through their logistics system.

Its sales in 2013 reached US$ 300 billion. The company has a broad range of digital businesses including activities similar to Amazon, eBay and PayPal. Its unique way of doing business, while maintaining synergy among its different investments to leverage the operation, also includes a "Cloud Computing and Internet Infrastructure" business line.

In China, approximately 80 percent of all mobile retail volume comes from the Alibaba site and the company utilizes 14 delivery partners employing 950,000 delivery personnel and dominates mobile commerce in that country.
In its vertical business model, Alibaba is a partial owner of Alipay, which processed 78.6 per cent of its transactions last year. Alibaba has a massive scale and an enormous market share, which has allowed it to experience continuous profit growth.

In Brazil, Privalia is an example of an e-commerce company following the same business model as Alibaba. It carries no inventory and works as an outlet for well-known fashion brands for men, women and children offering discounts of up to 70%. More than one thousand brands are available in its store. This online purchase club has been operating in Brazil since 2008 and has more than 6 million associates in Brazil and 15 million around the world, including Germany, Italy, Spain and Mexico.
Globally, 28% of its sales are made on mobile devices (smartphones and tablets). Its Privalia Mobile app is available for OS and Android platforms to make the

purchase experience easier and 1.8 million copies of this software have already been downloaded.

One of its differentials is its virtual store on Facebook known as "Fan Shop" with 2.6 million fans. Using this social network, the company has direct contact with its associates, offering exclusive promotions, purchase privileges and sharing suggestions and opinions. Part of its huge success can be attributed to its intensive and well-disseminated promotions, including between five and seven new campaigns launched every day for new offers and the design and performance of its site.

The companies above have guaranteed huge sales using a non-traditional business model where virtual retailers manage their own inventory, delivery processes and payments. Are the Alibaba and Privalia business models the best way to do business in a virtual environment?

E-Commerce Business Model

In the last twenty years, the internet has completely reshaped how people shop all over the world. It is common sense to actively surf the web to compare prices, research potential purchases on multiple websites, consult social networks and blogs for product reviews, and use different sources of information to purchase wherever is most convenient for them.

However, not all e-commerce experiences have been successful. Walmart's online volume for example, represents only 2% of its total global sales of US$ 473 billion. Amazon has annual sales revenues of US$ 75 billion, almost eight times more than Walmart. Theoretically, Walmart stores should be able to leverage their online business. They could work as storage and collection points for those customers who do not wish to receive the purchase at home. Today 19% of its physical store customers also buy on its site. The problem is that 53% of them also buy on Amazon.

As the world's largest retailer, Walmart is investing in technology to promote the intersection between its physical and digital business.

Neil Ashe, Walmart's global e-commerce president and chief executive officer states: *"There isn't a store customer or an online customer or a mobile customer. There's just one customer, and we're all committed to delivering one Walmart and one Sam's Club to that one customer,"* (MMR/March 31, 2014)

As two-thirds of the U.S. population live within five miles of a Walmart store, the company can use the stores as a delivery option for same-day shipping or in-store pickup.

Besides that, one quarter of Walmart customers have no credit cards or bank accounts. As such, they would be excluded from e-commerce if they did not have the chance to order online and pay with cash at a store.

Walmart is laying the logistical groundwork for the convergence between its brick-and-mortar stores and digital platform. That could give the company a competitive advantage customers something no one else can provide.

A recent study by Hahn and Kim (2009) found that consumers' trust in an off-line store was a significant predictor of both their confidence in shopping at the company's online store and their intention to search product information online using the company website. Consumers' trust in a retail brand significantly influences their intention to shop at the retailer's website.

Zentes et al (2007) state that retailer's stores brand can be considered to be their 'products'. It identifies a retailer's goods and services and differentiates them from those of competitors. A brand has its own characteristics or traits and they can be translated into a personality like a unique human being. There is a potential influence of brand personality on store loyalty (Zentes et al, 2008) because brands can convey symbolic associations.

Following the same line of thought, Angela Ahrendt, former Burberry CEO, was invited by Apple to develop a better link between virtual stores and the showrooms. In her opinion, in the next five years, there will be seven billion smartphones in the world willing to become potential customers. The internet page will be the store window and it must be developed to leverage sales.

Brand trust is the relationship between the confident expectations of the consumer and the resulting responsibility of the brand or retailer (Lau and Lee, 1999; Chaudhuri and Holbrook, 2001). If a customer has a positive behavior regarding an off-line retail brand, he or she is likely to be comfortable about shopping at the retailer's website. If the brand has a strong and positive reputation it will lead to brand repurchase, brand satisfaction and brand loyalty. Trust in a retailer is significantly related to intention to shop at the retailer's website (Loiacono, 2000; Liao and Cheung, 2001; Gommans et al., 2001).

Many analyses have been made on the conversion rate from search to sales and may suggest a product and brand assortment problem. Website design may also be improved to induce cross-selling, influencing buyers to increase their total purchase amount.

The best business model is clearly associated to company size.

An e-commerce business model demands scale in processing capability and an e-business model, focusing on customer needs, working intensively on marketing and communication.

The development of electronic commerce not only reduces shopping time, but also brings new possibilities of information technology in-house. Increasing customer requirements for product demand, giving rise to new products, which significantly contribute to a quick payback on investment (Němcová and Dvořák, 2011).

Dutch fashion store chain C&A is increasing its sales capillarity creating its own e-commerce that already serves 75 of the 5,570 cities in Brazil. Although it represents only 5% of its total revenue, average sales per customer is 50% higher.

Other companies that already have a huge number of franchisers and multi brand outlets, decided to apply the omni channel concept, selling on their virtual store. In order to avoid sales channel conflict, sales are delivered by the nearest store to the consumer. In this case, that store earns the respective profit on the sale. In case franchisers do not have the product available in store; they can offer it from the virtual store and still make some profit.

English company Farfetch has developed a partnership with a local fashion company and together they offer luxury brands like Yves Saint Laurent, Stella McCartney, Fendi, Moschino and Givenchy. Farfetch in Europe, has in its product portfolio more than eighty thousand items for female and male consumers.

The experience of e-commerce in Brazil

Due to the sales success of independent on-line websites, Brazilian brands have discovered that they must use the e-commerce channel in their strategy of multi-channel option to increase sales, complementing their market capillarity.

The strategy makes sense in a country like Brazil that represents today a consumer market of 210 million people. It is larger than the combined population of Spain and France.

On the other hand, today, 89% of the country's cities have less than fifty thousand inhabitants and, as average national income is low, especially in those smaller cities many types of stores would not reach their breakeven point making e-commerce the only way to serve consumers in those cities.

E-commerce volume grew significantly in Brazil over the last two years due to the increase in income, broad availability of internet infrastructure connections and increased sales of computers, smartphones, and tablets. Approximately ninety million Brazilians have bought on the internet at least once. Sales reached US$ 16 billion by the end of 2015, a fifteen percent increase over previous year volume. Fashion and accessories lead the sales ranking representing 18% of total volume followed by perfume and cosmetics (16%) and appliances (11%).

While the annual inflation rate in Brazil reached 10% in the last month of 2015, the price increase in the online environment was only 3.73%, probably due to the ease with which customers can compare prices.

There are 54 thousand e-commerce stores in Brazil and none of the fifty largest made any profit. This kind of business requires a heavy investment in technology, advertisement, logistics and reverse logistics, high financial cost and resources to combat fraud. More than one hundred million orders were placed on the Internet in 2015 and average purchase value was US$ 130.00.

Development of a new business model is in progress to convert a private e-commerce store like B2W (owner of Lojas Americanas, the largest department store chain in Brazil) or Cnova (Casino French Group owner of Pão de Açucar, the largest supermarket chain in Brazil) into a Market Place. Together they sell more than US$ 2 billion per year. In this new business model, their websites are transformed into market places where merchandising from different suppliers are offered and, once sold, delivered directly by them. The Market Place gets a 20% commission for sales avoiding the cost of logistics. Gross profit margin of a Market Place is higher than that on TV sets and refrigerators.

So far, those websites have registered great losses requiring frequent capital contributions from investors to keep operations running.

Amazon, the largest virtual shopping center in the world has gross profit margin of 35% higher than B2W (25%) and Cnova (13%). Rakuten, the leader in Japan has a 18% gross profit margin. Brazilian companies still have almost 90% of their total sales on their own products, lowering their margins. Some of the brands participating in these partnerships are Staples, Motorola, HP and Nike.

Nike opened its online store in Brazil in 2014 and has already become its second largest online store in the world.

Overall, e-commerce in Brazil tripled in the last four years and grew at a rate higher than the principal countries of Europe, the United States and Mexico. It has received investments from private equity companies of more than R$ 3.2 billion (US$ 1 billion) but most of the fifty largest online retailers are not making money and specialists say that some of them never will.

Although there is a strong demand for this sale channel, companies have not been able to balance sales revenue and operating costs. It is important to analyze what the best strategy of e-commerce in Brazil should be concerning business model, product assortment, logistics, advertising expenses, and payment terms.

Dafiti is a website, which sells over 75,000 apparel items. It obtained over US$300 million in capital from Rocket, a German private equity, and has more than US$ 500 million in sales revenue. However, the problem is that, the more it sells, the more money it loses. It has never been profitable in its four-year existence and specialists estimate a monthly loss of US$ 10 million.

The website recently merged its operation with four other online retailers to create the e-commerce company Global Fashion Group (GFG). Its controlling investors announced the merger: AB Kinnevikt of Sweden and Rocket Internet from Germany. This group consists of sites specialized in fashion from India (Jabong) Russia (Lamoda), Middle East (Namshi) and South East Asia and Australia (Zalora).

The intention is to develop a larger scale operation, to negotiate a larger budget with the internet media and obtain conditions that are more favorable.

This operation seems to confirm the concept that e-commerce is a large-scale operation which demands huge investments in technology, customer assistance, advertising and logistics. Creating synergy among these companies could lower costs and promote operating efficiency.

Is a large-scale business needed here, offering no room for small and medium size companies?

In recent years, the Brazilian market has witnessed the emergence of a large variety of online retail stores. Some examples are: furniture store Mobly, baby stores, pet shops and wine store "Wine.com.br" which has become the world's second largest. Some other entrepreneurs have invested in cosmetics, fashion apparel and real estate. The most recent movement has been in the stock brokerage business.

Most of them are not profitable, but nonetheless, some are worth a lot of money. Potential investors count on the long run to make money, or wait until the competition bothers someone larger and take over the competitor or go for an IPO.

International investors like JP Morgan Bank and Skype co-founder Niklas Zennström are leveraging the strong growth of e-commerce.

The idea is to replicate here the history of two American online retailers like Diapers.com, sold to Amazon for US$ 500 million in 2010 who also bought Zappos, a shoe store, for US$ 900 million in 2009. None of them had ever made a profit but became large enough to attract Amazon.

However, this strategy is difficult to follow in Brazil since the leaders in each niche face their own profitability problems. As there are many companies selling the same products on line, sellers must compete on price and offer free freight and payment terms in as many as twelve installments.

Those companies able to sell more and more with no profit will last longer. As the stock market has been undergoing a difficult period over the last three years, the IPO alternative has become a distant dream for most companies. Comprafacil.com was founded in 2003 and became the third largest electronic on line store before it went bankrupt in 2014.

Pressed by the risks and increasing debt, many companies tried to reduce their advertisement expenses, but their sales dropped immediately.

One alternative is to create a "fidelity club" where customers pay a fixed amount each month and can choose products on a regular basis. Wine.com.br adopted that strategy in 2013 and, for the first time, was able to make some profit. The company has fifty thousand subscribers. This club sells over 150,000 bottles a month.

A business model able to generate recurring revenue seems to be a way to guarantee enough funds to cover fixed costs and give longevity to the operation.

Those stores able to produce their own products or sell exclusive items can work with higher margins, giving them an advantage over competitors.

The main reasons given for losses are: low sales prices due to strong competition and the ease of comparison to other websites, high delivery costs, heavy investment in advertising, and financial cost of consumers purchase on credit and high level of fraud.

Netshoes, the largest online sporting goods store was founded in 2000 and through 2014 was still unable to make profit even with sales over US$ 500 million. New investments have been necessary to keep the wheel turning. Morgan Stanley investment bank was hired to find an investor interested in buying the business, but were unsuccessful.

The combination of loss and poor cash flow can lead to conflict between entrepreneurs and investors.

There is also a great opportunity in Brazil to develop a virtual environment for B2B (Business to Business). Different from United States, this is still a very incipient business demanding new platforms to link the industry, wholesalers and retailers in this huge country. Two platforms linking the industry to retailers in the fashion business have succeeded: *e-Moda Showroom* and *Moda em Atacado*.

Internet Price Strategy

Online retailers must take price-splitting decisions regarding shipping and handling fees. Some of them show customers a price split between product price and a separate delivery surcharge while others prefer to offer free shipping using a single-price format where the product price already includes shipping (Mehmet Gumus, Wonseok and Saibal, 2013).

Two considerations must be made here: the first refers to the customer's perception of product cost, the other is that e-commerce related shipping, and handling costs can account for more than 30% of the total cost in a number of sectors such as groceries and toys (Barsh et al. 2000 apud Mehmet Gumus, Wonseok and Saibal, 2013). In Brazil, as only 16% of the roads are paved, therefore this cost can be an important issue.

Online retailers must carefully trade off the negative impact of delivery-related expenses on their total costs against the positive effect of not charging customers for delivery expenses. It is not very easy to decide on the optimal pricing strategy based on the characteristics of the products being sold by the retailer.

Better supply chain network design and inventory management can certainly reduce shipping and handling costs for online retailers.

Internet safety

E-commerce not only has tremendous potential for growth but also poses unique challenges for both current players and new entrants. According to Saini and Johnson (2005) some capabilities act as drivers of firm performance in e-commerce: information technology capability, strategic flexibility, and trust-building capability.

Concerning trust building Kwon and Lee (2003) found empirical evidence of an inverse relationship between security concerns and Internet purchases. They also found that providing alternative off-line payment methods reduces security concerns and therefore promotes on-line purchases.

Security is still a significant issue for today's Internet shoppers despite the introduction of e-cash, encryption and decryption technologies. It is critical for Internet retailers to dispel consumers' negative attitudes about the safety of using credit cards on-line.

The Internet retail industry has introduced various methods such as encryption technologies attempting to prevent fraud such as stolen credit card numbers and identity theft, one of the main costs for on-line retailers on line. Security issues and consumer protection has been extensively discussed by specialists in Brazil since payments using mobile phones represents today eight percent of total sales, but specialists forecast a participation of 15% in the next five years. New technologies such as Chip&Pin and NFC (Near Field Communication) are being introduced in order to increase consumer protection needs when using their credit cards. The reluctance to use credit cards for on-line purchases is one of the primary obstacles to the future growth of Internet shopping.

Lack of trust is one of the most frequently cited reasons for consumers not purchasing from Internet vendors due to anonymity, lack of control and possible opportunism (Grabner-Krauter and Kaluschab, 2003). Sensitive personal information must be supplied such as mailing address, telephone number and credit card number, making risk and trust crucial elements of electronic commerce.

Internet Retail companies must necessarily focus on measures and policies to build and maintain consumer trust.

According to Shim et al. (2001), transaction service such as payment security, privacy, safety, product guarantees, and minimal cost/time for returns affected consumers' intentions to use the Internet for purchasing.

Analyzing from the retailers point of view, Brazil has a high rate of fraud and, according to CyberSource Brasil, seven percent of total sales online are rejected by the sellers in Brazil due to suspected fraud equivalent to US$ 110 million. In United States this represents 2.7% of total sales. Local legislation says that, when a purchase is made online, retailers assume responsibility for any losses. If a purchase is made in an onsite store, the credit card administrator is the one who will assume any possible losses on the transaction.

This kind of threat adds an extra cost to the operation. The huge online sites have teams dedicated to making manual reviews to ensure that transactions are not fraudulent in 31% of the cases. Nonetheless, 1.08% of total sales are identified as fraudulent after the respective transactions have been completed. Considering that, 104 million transactions were made in 2015 that means tremendous operational costs for companies. That risk may increase with the adoption of mobile devices by the population.

Value Perception on Internet shopping

Many studies have covered the possible variables related to value perception in e-commerce environment. Some of them, in addition to security on the Internet (already discussed) are: Influence of Friends and Advertisements, Convenience of the Internet, Brand admiration, Better price offering, Ease in the Ordering and Delivery process, Return Policy and Quality of information online.

A previous study reported a strong relationship between a website's information quality and customer usage of interactive features on impulse e-shopping purchase behavior (Lin and Chuan, 2013). According to the authors of the study, information quality has a direct influence on impulse purchase on internet, but perceived trust and use of interactive feature were not supported.

As many consumers use the Internet as a source of information this affects the intention to purchase through this channel (Shim et al.2000). When consumers are satisfied with the information provided by the retailer on-line, they are more likely to make a purchase. For web retailers it is easier to provide customers with specific and up-to-date information about the product on a 24hour/7day base (Silverman, 1998).

Other advantages offered by technology are the ease to improve online product displays and real-time customer service, which apparently lead to more sales (Paderni et al., 2005).

From the shopping process, people derive several different outcomes such as products, information, and pleasure (Lee and Johnson, 2002). Shopping includes both information searching behavior and purchasing behavior.

The main business of many sites is to offer the customers the ease of viewing the large amount of information available and comparing products and prices on-line.

The interactive nature of the Internet is a crucial element in online consumer decision-making (Shim et al., 2001). When a consumer has enough information about a product's price, size, color, function, it is easier to make a decision and Shim et al. (2001) proposed that intention to search for information online is a predictor of an intention to buy online.

Customer perceived value is subjective in nature with a number of components that contribute to an evaluative judgment. There is a relationship between store perceived value and customer attitude, which is an important determinant of customer loyalty. A study by Ruiz-Molina and Gil-Saura (2008) concluded that store perceived value has a strong influence on both customer attitude and, consequently, store loyalty.

Brakus et al (2009) had related the brand experience to store loyalty. The shopping and service experience includes not only utilitarian attributes but also hedonic dimensions, such as feelings, pleasure, and can be affected by marketing communication. Brand connection can lead to involvement related to values, interests and needs.

Innovativeness is part of consumers' shopping behavior. To understand that it is important to help online retailers learn how to convert browsers into purchasers to capture revenues (Ha and Stoel, 2004).

Innovativeness includes the adoption of new products and Goldsmith et al.'s study (1987) showed that women are likely to be more innovative than men are. The basic proposal of fashion apparel is to innovate for every season and shopping on the Internet is a new sales channel for most consumers in Brazil.

For security reasons or due to difficulty in trying on apparel products, consumers may choose to search for information online as a more convenient way, but still prefer to visit stores for shopping. The in-store experience cannot be replicated on the Internet, but other benefits may be added to this new channel like the use of avatars to help consumers to see how clothes will fit.

Brand involvement may give the consumer the perception of innovativeness and Michaelidou and Dibb (2008) considered the potential influence on involvement with the choice of a shopping channel for the purchase of particular products. Even on the Internet, sensorial experience is important to consumers.

Customer satisfaction leads to perceived service quality and, consequently, service value. Perceived service quality is defined as the customer's assessment of the service's overall excellence or superiority (Zeithaml 1988).

Bolton and Drew (1991) say that customer assessments of service value are positively related to their evaluations of service quality. Perceptions of performance exert a direct influence on customer satisfaction and customers' expectation will depend on their tastes, characteristics, personal needs and word-of-mouth past experiences. The gap between expectations and perceptions leads to satisfaction or dissatisfaction.

Customer satisfaction can be related to a specific transaction or an overall evaluation of a particular service's quality. When considering consumer behavior, the higher the level of satisfaction, the greater the chance to generate purchase intentions and behavior.

Another variable considered by shoppers in their service evaluation is delivery-time–related information, which is directed related to stock availability and shipping/handling cycle (Park and Kim, 2007). Reduction of waiting time for Internet products is considered important to consumers and contributes to their value perception.

Product Assortment on the internet

Concerning product assortment, in developing a successful e-commerce strategy it is important to focus on the experience of the current and potential customers. To do that, it is necessary to consider which advice is being used to access the site. According to Faisal Masud, vice president of global e-commerce at Staples, as smartphones or tablets became a moving store in customers' hands, good product selection, low price, quick delivery and clear return policy have become the main issues for business success (Lundquist, 2014).

Walmart, for example, included grocery delivery business in 2012 and food contributed more than half of the retailer's annual sales.

The decision on the breadth and depth of product assortment on the internet is another consideration to be made. While "bricks and mortar" retail establishments live with the physical constraints of carrying large inventories and limited space available to display products that constraint does not exist in a virtual environment. For most retailers, the Pareto rule or, more simply, the "80/20" rule is suitable. That means in practice that businesses will focus on the 20 percent of products that produce 80 percent of all revenue. Companies could reasonably ignore products that were not "popular" as they represent a relatively small proportion of the total sales. Besides that, due to a store's limited ability to service a specific regional market, there is no demand for a large number of products.

In the internet business, where theoretically there is no physical restraint on inventory breadth and depth, the "long tail "concept may be applied. This term was coined by Anderson (2004) to describe his observations of the impact of the internet on the demand curve for products sold electronically.

This theory defends the idea that the typical demand curve is characterized by high demand for a few items (the short head) and reduced demand for a larger variety of products (the long tail).

The "short head" and "long tail" describe the statistical distribution of sales in which a few items occur frequently (the short head) and a large number of items occur less frequently.

On the internet, this concept may work in a different way. As on the internet, transaction costs are low, inventory can be unconstrained and market reach extensive, online retailers could take advantage of the "long tail" demand curve. The internet has shown that, under certain circumstances, the "long tail" has become longer, thicker, and more profitable than previously understood. Offering products on the internet that are not easily found on traditional retailers can offer a competitive advantage to online businesses to ensure better profit margins.

The combination of high turnover items that have the power to attract customers with exclusive and high margin items could be a good way of making money.

This strategy could settle or at least mitigate the "unprofitable game" that most e-commerce businesses in Brazil have been playing. The concentration of product assortment on high sales items can compromise companies' profitability (Day Ward, Choi and Zhao, 2011), while the 80 percent on the products can always contribute to higher revenue for the online market (Anderson, 2006).

According to Anderson (2006), three forces reinforce the long tail concept:

1-In the internet environment it is easier to use tools that enable companies to establish a web presence and present their products; 2-Consumers can access products in an easy and inexpensive way; 3-Sites are able to introduce customers to newly available but scarce goods, driving demand to the tail. Google and Trip Advisor are examples of services that have the potential to stimulate niche demand, the basic characteristic of a long tail strategy.

E-commerce demands a massive scale and costly operations. Some virtual retailers have been successful in the process of mitigating risk and controlling operational costs. Due to the ease of price comparison, companies must offer competitive prices, something, which prevents them from making higher profits. On the other hand, differentiation by product assortment applying the "long tail" concept" and using other companies' inventories to offer exclusive products with better profit margin, could be a good option to conciliate the offer of a broader assortment without increasing inventory cost. The business model creating recurring revenue on the development of "fidelity club" could also minimize the business risk.

Due to strong competition, the business demands intensive communication and the use of social media could be the lowest cost alternative.

Customers' value perception is also related to information quality, ease of ordering, return policy, short delivery time and payment security. All those attributes demand investment in technology and operational structure. In order to minimize this investment, outsourcing those services, especially payment security and financing operation, providing a long-term installment and delivery process including reverse logistic cost, could be a good alternative as long as the synergy among these elements is preserved. Alibaba has already promoted that business model, maintaining those activities concentrated in specialized companies, but holding equity ownership in those companies.

Another important consideration in the business model strategy is the merging between the "bricks and mortar" store and the e-commerce operation. The joint operation can be used to leverage sales, reduce inventory volume and shipping and handling cycle.

So far, the e-commerce business model that has shown itself to be profitable, has been based on the cost reduction strategy, acting as an intermediary which promotes and sells merchandise from some other company's inventory. Logistics, customer financing cost, and risk of fraud cost have been outsourced. Product exclusivity has had to be focused in order to increase profit margin.

For further study, it would be useful to investigate how large the market has to be to allow e-commerce companies to earn money based on operating scale. As mentioned previously, some companies in US were sold to larger companies after many years of losses because they became large enough to affect the business of important market players. In Brazil, although this has already taken place in the "bricks and mortar" retail business, it is unlikely to occur in the internet environment.

Communication Strategy

Over the last ten years, while total population increased 12%, some regions such as the North and Central West grew 23% and 21% respectively. This phenomenon of migration to smaller cities has increased in recent years. As of last year, 77.6 million people (39.4% of the population) did not live in the same city where they were born. This movement has brought opportunities to companies like

MCDONALD'S and large supermarket chains, which have been reducing the size of their stores to fit in the new markets.

Another important consideration in product development and communication strategy is racial distribution. 46.2% of the Brazilian population is white and virtually all the rest is afro descendent. This balance changes dramatically in some regions: while in the South 76.8% of the population is white, in the North this percentage drops to 22%.

RACE DISTRIBUTION BY REGION

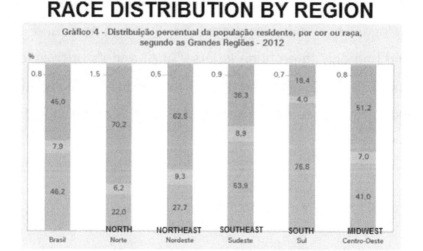

Race distribution by region

This new racial distribution in Brazil, very different especially between the South and North regions, demands the use of different elements in product and communication. Real cases have proven to be successful offering different products, especially for hair and skin treatment.

Besides that, it is important to highlight the fact that culture may vary greatly from one region to another, demanding the use of local slang and regional expressions.

Another concern related to communication strategy is the low level of education. 8.7% of the population is illiterate and 18.3% have less than four years of formal education. Despite this handicap, these people are consumers. Unilever has developed a laundry detergent for this segment and the brand had only three huge letters, "ALA" and its price is less than US$ 0.50. The company followed MC DONALD's principle that uses its big yellow "M" which can be identified even by children.

Final Comments

As Bruno Ferrari stated in his article (2013), since the 1960's Brazil has not been considered a poor country, but is stuck in "the average income trap". In comparing Brazil and South Korea, he notes that both countries had an average per capita income of five thousand dollars in the 1970s. In Brazil, this income slightly more than doubled to eleven thousand, while in South Korea it soared to US$ 30,000. In forty years Korea joined the group of the richest countries in world, while Brazil, although no longer a poor country, has not achieved the status of a developed country.

Brazil has had significant improvement in its political, economic and social development, but this has not been sufficient to meet the needs of its vast and growing population and latent demand. New actions must consider multiple dimensions.

In 2008, the country was not deeply affected by the global financial crisis.   Now, Brazil's economic development has reached a point of inflection and this time has come to accelerate productivity growth and deliver higher living standards. Focus on education and training to develop human capital is a big issue.

Considering its average low income and the great potential of consumption leveraged by the two hundred and ten million inhabitants, it is relevant to find the way for a successful business. A small but very rich percentage of population, geographically concentrated, is willing to spend on luxury products, making the country a very attractive market for this segment.

On the other hand, approximately 210 million people are potential consumers for companies willing to operate on the average price level. These companies have to be aware of what kind of operation to adopt in order to avoid the high financial and logistics costs and high taxes applied on manufacturing products. Partnerships, distributed inventory, direct sales, franchising, and e-commerce may be some of the business model solutions to face such a high potential market but with so many challenges.

Many business opportunities are still in the process of development in the domestic market. Those opportunities can be leveraged by redirecting trade policy to achieve closer integration with major markets.

Few other countries offer such a large domestic market with its vast and expanding consumption. Additionally, Brazil has a demographic bonus. Most of its population is working age and at the peak consumption period.

It is the world's seventh-largest economy, but ranks only 95th in GDP per capita. On the other hand, the low level of sophistication of the Brazilian basic shopping basket offers plenty of opportunities for consumer goods industry. The huge aspiring middle class of 120 million people can be a source of sustainable growth. Besides that, a group of 40 million people on the bottom line of the pyramid can be favored by the economy and attracted to the consumer market.

Management inefficiency must be solved and the infrastructure shortfall is still a major issue preventing the country from growing.

There was a dramatic reduction in the official poverty rate driven in large part by federal social programs. The political party in power for the last twelve years has promoted growth-stimulating demand. This model has lost its momentum and consumption is reaching its limit since many Brazilian consumers rely on credit for cosmetics, food and beverage and many other consumer products. Now it is time to invest in the supply chain, supporting it with better logistic infrastructure, generating new jobs, investing in human capital to support productivity, developing a regulatory stability and encouraging entrepreneurship to sustain long-term growth.

This strategy possibly would help to ease the heavy burden for consumers that restrict consumption. That is also an incentive to the "gray" (informal) market that attempts to avoid taxes and gain cost advantage.

Barriers must be removed and competition encouraged in areas like energy, telecommunication, agriculture, transportation, infrastructure, supplementary health care, complementary pension plans, Insurance, consumer products and the construction industry. Investment in technology is also crucial to Brazil's competitiveness.

It is essential to redesign growth policies to compete in a more global and intensive economy. Of course it is necessary to lower the so-called "Brazil cost" (cost of doing business in Brazil) to improve competitiveness and attract investment. Today, high taxes and tariffs, inadequate ports, railways, roads and slow-moving bureaucracy increase the cost of business and this cost is passed on to consumers who pay high prices in the local market. In 2014 Brazilian tourists spent US$ 9.3 billion abroad while foreign tourists spent only US$ 2.7 billion in Brazil.

One of the main important facts to be highlighted is the rapid regional development-taking place in the country. The new business centers have brought new jobs and new consumers to the market. They now demand local offer of products and services. E-commerce, franchising and direct sales are supporting that necessity.

Some challenges have to be faced to serve this promising, but risky market. An appropriate business model is required to fit the market and achieve volumes above the breakeven point. The North and Central West regions are the main areas to be highlighted. Millions of new consumers have begun to increase their spending, especially in medium-sized urban areas that today offer good business opportunities.

There are plenty of opportunities in several segments. Companies like Kopenhagen, a chocolate retail chain, have been working with two distinctive brands to attend different social classes. Recently, they made a deal to represent Lindt, the Swiss company, in Brazil and some stores have already been opened. Other companies have followed the same strategy, making money in both sides of this huge consumer group.

BNDES – Brazil's National Bank of Economic and Social Development, one of the largest development banks in the world, has helped finance most of the investments made in the last decades. Now it is the turning point. It is necessary to attract productive and not only speculative investment.

The growth drivers used thus far now have reached their limits. It is time to develop a new sustainable growth model, based on infrastructure.

There is no ideal or long-lasting strategy. The essence of strategy is to choose activities that are different from rivals. Being the first is a great advantage since being the best does not last for long.

References

ABRATE, Graziano; CAPRIELLO, Antonella and FRAQUELLI, Giovanni. When quality signals talk: Evidence from the Turin hotel industry. Tourism Management 32 (2011) 912 e 921

APPLEGATE, L. M. (1999) "Electronic commerce". In Richard, C. Dorf (ed),
The Technology Management Handbook (11.22-30). USA: CRC Press LLC.
Anuário Exame 2014-2015- October 0214

AREND, Richard J The business model: Present and future-- beyond a skeumorph. Strategic Organization September 2013 p:390-402

ARNOULD, Eric J. and MOHR, Jakki J. Dynamic Transformations for Base-of-the-Pyramid Market Clusters. *Journal of the Academy of Marketing Science,*. Volume 33, No. 3, pages 254-274. Jun 16, 2005

ATSMON,Yuval, KERTESZ, Ari, and VITTAL, Ireena Is your emerging-market strategy local enough? The diversity and dynamism of China, India, and Brazil defy any one-size-fits-all approach. But by targeting city clusters within them, companies can seize growth opportunities. McKinsey Quarterly April, 2011

BADEN-FILLER, Charles and MANGEMATIN, Vincent. Business models: A challenging agenda. Strategic Organization, November 2013,pp 418-427

BARNEY, J. Firm resources and sustained competitive advantage. Journal of Management, (1991). 17, 99-120.
BIGGART, Nicole Woolsey. The Creative-Destructive Process of Organizational Change: The case of the Post Office. Administrative Science Quarterly, September 1977, volume 22

Brazilian Association of Distance Learning – Analytic report of distance learning in Brazil, 2012

CASADESUS-Masanell, R. and RICART, J. (2010) "From Strategy to Business Models and onto Tactics," Long Range Planning 43(2/3): 195–215.

CLINTON, Bill. Giving – How each of us can change the world. Alfred A. Knopf, 2007

COLLINS, Jim and PORRAS, Jerry I. Built to Last, successful habits of visionary companies. Harper Collins Publishers, 2002

DAY, Jonathon; WARD, Liz; CHOI,Suh-hee and ZHAO, Chen (Zara).
Catching the long tail: competitive advantage through distribution strategy. Journal of Hospitality and Tourism Technology, Vol. 2 No. 3, 2011 pp. 204-215.

DHLIWAYO, Shepherd. Entrepreneurship and Competitive Strategy: An Integrative Approach. The Journal of Entrepreneurship 23(1), 2014, pp 115–135.

FELLENSTEIN, C. & WOOD, R. (2000) Exploring E-commerce, Global E-business and E-Societies. New Jersey, USA: Prentice Hall PTR

FERRARI, Bruno. " O Brasil está preso na armadilha da renda média". Magazine EXAME 07/08/2013

GUETTA, Alain; VON JESS, Ana Cristina et al. Franchising – Learn from the experts. ABF, Rio de Janeiro, 2013.

HAMMER, Michael. Mudança Profunda: como a inovação operacional pode transformar sua empresa. Harvard Business Review, Abril 2004 p.47 -54

HILLETOFTH, Per; HILMOLA, Olli-Pekka and CLAESSON,Frida. In-transit distribution strategy: solution for European factory competitiveness? Industrial Management & Data Systems Vol. 111 No. 1, 2011 pp. 20-40.

IRELAND , R. Duane, HOSKISSON, HITT. The Management of Strategy 8th edition

IVEROTH, Einar ; WESTELIUS, Alf ; PETRI, Carl-Johan; OLVE, Nils-Goran; COSTER, Mathias; NILSSON, Fredrik. How to differentiate by price: Proposal for a five-dimensional model. European Management Journal (2013) 31, 109– 123.

KAUFFELD, Rich; SAUER, Johan and BERGSON, Sara. Partners at the Point of Sale. Strategy + Business – Columbia Business School, August 29, Autumn 2007 / Issue 48.

KOTLER, Philip – What is Strategy? – Harvard Business Review, November-December1996 – pp-61-79

LEHNER, Othmar, KAMSIKAS, Juha. Opportunity Recognition in Social Entrepreneurship - A Thematic Meta Analysis. Journal of Entrepreneurship March 2012 vol. 21 no. 1 25-58

LI,Jianxiang; CHEN, Haoxun and CHU, Feng. Performance evaluation of distribution strategies for the inventory routing problem. European Journal of Operational Research 202 (2010) 412–419

LIAO, Chin-Nung. Fuzzy analytical hierarchy process and multi-segment goal programming applied to new product segmented underprice strategy. Computers & Industrial Engineering 61 (2011) 831–841

MARTINS, Cesar et all. McKinsey Global Institute – Connecting Brazil to the world: A path to inclusive growth – May 2014.

MOLLA, Alemayehu and LICKERPaul S. E-commerce systems success: An attempt to extend and respecify the Delone and Maclean model of IS success. Journal of Electronic Commerce Research, 2001.

PALICH, Leslie and GOMEZ-MEJIA, Luis R. Theory of Global Strategy and Firm Efficiencies: Considering the Effects of Cultural Diversity. Journal of Management, 1999, Vol. 25, No. 4, 587–606

PARR, J. B. (1978) Regional competition , growth pole policy and public intervention, in: W. BUHR and P. FRIEDRICH (Eds) Konkurren z zwischen kleinen Regionen : Competition Among Small Regions , pp. 163-177.

PARR John B. Growth-pole Strategies in Regional Economic Planning: A Retrospective View: Part 1. Origins and Advocacy. *Urban Studies, Vol. 36, No. 7, 1195-1215, 1999*

NGUYEN, Hanh, STUCHTEY, STUCHTEY, Martin and SILS, Markus. Remaking the industrial economy. A regenerative economic model—the circular economy—is starting to help companies create more value while reducing their dependence on scarce resources. McKinsey Quarterly February, 2014.

SAKO, Mari. Business Models for Strategy and Innovation Technology Strategy and Management. Communications of the acm | July 2012 | vol. 55 | no. 7

STEAD, Jean Garner and STEAD, W. Edward. The Coevolution of Sustainable Strategic Management in the Global Marketplace. *Organization Environment June,* 2013 p: 162-183

SHAW, Margaret. Positioning and Price: Merging Theory, Strategy, and Tactics. Journal of Hospitality & Tourism Research 1992, Volume 15 Number2.

SIMÕES, Raphael. "O inimigo virou sócio na busca por novos resultados", Magazine EXAME 27/06/ 2012.

SYMONDS, Matt Interview with Bill
Drayton, Pioneer of
Social Entrepreneurship: 7 Questions to
Find out If You're Ready to Be an

Entrepreneur In 2015.

Leadership 9/30/2013

THACKERAY, Rosemary and BROWN, Kelli R. McCormack, Creating Successful Price and Placement Strategies for Social Marketing. Social Marketing and Health Communication. March 2010 Vol. 11, No. 2, 166-168.

STEVERMAN, Ben from Bloomberg. Emergentes valem o risco, Valor Newspaper, January, 2015, page D2

TAYLOR, Valerie A. and BEARDEN, William O. The Effects of Price on Brand Extension Evaluations: The Moderating Role of Extension Similarity. Journal of the Academy of Marketing Science Spring, 2002. P:130-140

THACKERAY, Rosemary and BROWN, Kelli R. McCormack. Creating Successful Price and Placement Strategies for Social Marketing. Health Promotion Practice. March 2010, p: 165-168

VALOR Setorial Franquias – May 2014

VALOR Setorial Saúde – August 2014

VALOR Setorial Agronegócio – September, 2014

YAN, Ruiliang; MYERS, Chris Anthony and WANG, John Price strategy, information sharing, and firm performance in a market channel with a dominant retailer. Journal of Product & Brand Management 21/6 (2012) 475–485

YU, Kangkang, CADEAUX, Jack and SONG, Hua. Alternative forms of fit in distribution flexibility strategies. International Journal of Operations & Production Management Vol. 32 No. 10, 2012 pp. 1199-1227.

ZEITHAML, V. (1988). Consumer perceptions of price, quality, and value: a means-end model and synthesis of evidence. The Journal of Marketing, 52(3), 2–22.

ZENG, Chenhang. OPTIMAL ADVANCE SELLING STRATEGY UNDER
PRICE COMMITMENT. Pacific Economic Review, 18: 2 (2013)

ZOTT,Christoph and AMIT, Raphael. The fit between Product Market Strategy and Business Model implications for

Firm Performance. Strategic Management Journal Strat. Mgmt. J., 29: 1–26 (2008)

ZOTT, Christoph, AMIT, Raphael and MASSA, Lorenzo. The Business Model: Recent Developments and Future Research. Journal of Management July 2011 vol. 37 no. 4 1019-1042

ZOTT, Christoph and AMIT, Raphael. The business model: A theoretically anchored robust construct for strategic analysis Strategic Organization November, 2013 p: 403-411.

ZWASS, Vladimir. Electronic Commerce: Structures and Issues. International Journal of Electronic Commerce, Volume 1, Number 1, Fall, 1996, pp. 3 - 23.

Made in the USA
Las Vegas, NV
19 March 2021